THE GOOD COOK'S BOOK OF

Tomatoes

THE GOOD COOK'S BOOK OF

Tomatoes

WITH MORE THAN 200 RECIPES

Michele Anna Jordan

Foreword by Flo Braker

Illustrations by Michel Stong

ADDISON-WESLEY PUBLISHING COMPANY
Reading, Massachusetts   Menlo Park, California   New York
Don Mills, Ontario   Wokingham, England   Amsterdam   Bonn
Sydney   Singapore   Tokyo   Madrid   San Juan
Paris   Seoul   Milan   Mexico City   Taipei

Library of Congress Cataloging-in-Publication Data
Jordan, Michele Anna.
The good cook's book of tomatoes : with more than 200 recipes /
Michele Anna Jordan; foreword by Flo Braker;
illustrations by Michel Stong.
p.   cm.
Includes bibliographical references and index.
ISBN 0-201-62711-6
1. Cookery (Tomatoes)   2. Tomatoes.   I. Title.
TX803.T6J67 1995
641.6′5642—dc20   94-46976
                                                      CIP

Cover and interior illustrations by Michel Stong
Cover design by Diana Coe
Text design by Karen Savary
Set in 11-point Weiss by Carol Woolverton Studio

1 2 3 4 5 6 7 8 9 10-DOH-9998979695
First printing, April 1995

*This one's for two of my favorite tomato lovers,
James Carroll and John Boland*

CONTENTS

RECIPES BY COURSE

FOREWORD

For as long as I can remember, I've had a passion for food. For me, cooking is one of life's great pleasures, and I believe that most of us want to feel relaxed and knowledgeable in the kitchen. Many of us want to cook with inspiration as well.

Just as an artist experiences a sense of well-being and an edge of excitement when sitting down with brushes, paints, and palette to create a new work, a cook likes to feel both confident and full of ideas when he or she opens the pantry, reaches for an apron, and begins cooking.

My idea of a great cookbook is one that, on opening it, I want to take to a quiet corner to read and savor, because I know immediately that it's going to give me lots of information, some new skills, and lasting inspiration.

Michele Jordan has written three such books: *The Good Cook's Book of Oil & Vinegar*, *The Good Cook's Book of Mustard*, and now *The Good Cook's Book of Tomatoes*. Her approach is to guide us to explore every facet of each essential ingredient in her grand collections of innovative recipes so that we can duplicate as well as experiment and to encourage us to use what we've learned.

Today, all across America, consumers have an embarrassment of riches. So many new and unfamiliar vinegars, oils, mustards, and tomatoes are available, that just shopping for a recipe can be a challenge. Michele gives us exactly the information we need to make intelligent choices so that we can work with these ingredients easily and skillfully and use them as a springboard for our own culinary creations.

Michele's three volumes are not just cookbooks to be quickly scanned in order to decide what to whip up for a meal. Instead, each book treats a particular ingredient so thoroughly that in the end you can almost taste the recipes as you read them, and then go on to create countless variations of your own.

This fine trilogy of companion books weaves the vibrant tastes, textures, and aromas of everyday essential ingredients into well-organized information that appeals to the novice as well as to the experienced home cook. Each book begins with some historical, botanical, and commercial background on the ingredient, and even addresses pertinent health issues. A section called "The Annotated Pantry" includes Michele's personal comments and notes. Her recipes follow, and they are easy-to-prepare contemporary dishes that guarantee delicious results for every course of a meal.

Michele's glossary, "Tasting" section, and sample forms for conducting your own tastings are invaluable resources. Her easy-to-follow instructions on how to conduct comparative tastings educate your palate and give you faith in your own judgment. After all, that's what good cooking is all about—taste.

For me, though, perhaps the greatest pleasure in reading any one of the "Good Cook's Books" is that Michele brings life to the ingredients that we tend to take for granted. After reading one of these books you will never again underestimate the power of a simple ingredient. Moreover, you'll want the entire series close to you in the kitchen as handy references to use again and again. Michele's passion jumps off each page and entices you to taste, experiment, and cook. Three cheers for "The Good Cook's Books: Oil & Vinegar! Mustard! Tomatoes!"

FLO BRAKER
PALO ALTO, 1995

ACKNOWLEDGMENTS

John Boland and James Carroll moved to Sonoma County in 1989, when they purchased *The Paper*, a small alternative newspaper that had been limping along for about ten years. With John as publisher and Jim as editor, they transformed the publication and in the process transformed me, too. I became a contributor in 1990 with my column "The Jaded Palate," which I had been writing for another publication since 1986. Soon thereafter I became restaurant critic, and began writing features on a wide range of topics, from genetically engineered tomatoes and former CIA agents to bats, books, and music. In 1994, *The Paper* was rechristened *The Sonoma County Independent*, I was made contributing editor for food and wine, and at the end of the year John left the day-to-day operations of the paper, having seen it through its painful years of growth and expansion. Jim remains as editor. It is difficult, without sounding maudlin or hyperbolic, to say how thoroughly my life has been transformed by my years writing for the *Independent*. But I can say that I consider myself blessed among writers, for Jim is a brilliant and inspiring editor. And so, to Jim and John, *thanks for finding each other, Sonoma County, and me: this is for you.*

Many people offered valuable information, advice, and technical assistance, as well as an abundance of tomatoes, as

I wrote this book. Special thanks to Charley Rick of UC Davis; Carolyn Coughlin, marketing coordinator for Muir Glen Tomatoes; Carolyn Hayworth of Calgene; William Toll of Taste of the World; Martha Johnson of Eden Foods; Jeff Dawson of Grandview Farms; Bonnie and Malcolm Yuill-Thornton of Dragonfly Farms; Leonard Diggs of The Farmery; Ruth Waltenspiel of Timber Crest Farms; Ron Tanner of the National Association of the Specialty Food Trade; and Robert Ambrose of the Tomato Club.

I also want to acknowledge the tremendous support of my assistants, Lesa Tanner and Betty Ellsworth, who keep me sane; my agents Angela Miller and Betsy Amster; my friend and copy editor Liesel Hofmann; my editor at Addison-Wesley, Elizabeth Carduff; Pat Jalbert and Jen Colton, also of Addison-Wesley; Christine Palmer-Persen and Steve Axelrod; Tom Simoneau of Windsor Vineyards; Scott Murray of KRCB-FM; George Hower of *The Press Democrat*; Steve Garner of KSRO-AM; Tom Menrath and Greg Reisinger of the Olive Hill Oil Company; and Sidney Moore of Sutton Place Gourmet. And to Ridgley Evers and his exceptional new DaVero extra-virgin olive oil, which I eagerly anticipate enjoying with summer's first tomatoes—thanks for doing it and good luck!

I also want to extend a huge thank you to California State Senator Mike Thompson and his wife Jan Thompson, for their astonishing efforts and generosity in opening their home for a dream-come-true dinner party (wherein an old Sicilian recipe—*Gudene*, which you will find in this book—was revived and served to one of my only cultural heroes, Francis Ford Coppola, and his wife Eleanor). Special thanks, as well, to Mike's secretary, Nancy Lynott, for arranging things. And to Lee Engdahl, for honoring my flamboyant request for a letterpress menu of the dinner—thank you!

And finally, love, hugs, and kisses to my family and friends, old and new, who continue to make life good: especially, my daughters Gina and Nicolle; David Siracusa, his cousin Paul Carrara, and their new restaurant, Sapphire Mynx; Elizabeth Ramsey, Daniel Patterson, and their new restaurant, Babette's; Garrick Maul; Bob Sala; Julieta Leal Weiss; Ginny Stanford; Sandy Nelson; Susan and Larry Watson; Andy Ross of Cody's Books; Lou Preston of Preston Vineyards and Winery; Rob Cole and Café This; Leslie and Brian, who were married at my home just shortly before I finished the book; and Guy and Mary, again, and always; and once again, artist Michel Stong and her family, for absolutely everything.

INTRODUCTION

I

"What's the sequel to *Mustard* going to be?" a friend asked. "Ketchup?"

Very funny, I thought, but admitted that the answer is yes, *sort of*, even though the sweet pungent tomato condiment we call ketchup was a walnut-based sauce in Europe centuries ago. Today, *ketchup* is synonymous with *tomato*.

The tomato has been one of my favorite foods since I can remember. The memory of each summer of my childhood is fragrant with red and golden vine-ripened tomatoes, many of them from my grandfather's garden, others from a farm stand on the edge of town. I ate them with abandon, took them for granted, considered them an essential fact of life, like rain in the winter or my birthday in July. It never occurred to me that a simple tomato, pure and sweet and silky, would ever be out of my grasp. That realization would come later, when I was a young mother and garden-grown tomatoes were harder and harder to come by. In the days of youthful abundance, they were simply a part of summer, like cherries, watermelon, and dark, juicy nectarines.

My most vivid memories of tomatoes are connected to bouts of childhood illnesses, when I would rest propped up on the couch with thick, deep pillows, pampered with juices and stories, but most of all, tempted with whatever I was willing to eat. My favorite sickbed meal consisted of tomatoes and beef, more suited perhaps to a Chicago steak house, but there you have it. A little steak was broiled very rare and cut into small pieces. Next to it would be similarly cut pieces of tomato, a little salt sprinkled over the whole affair. I ate with limpid pleasure and drank the delicious juices that collected in the center of the plate. As I write of it now, I can nearly taste the sharp, acidic, salty pleasure.

Perhaps because tomatoes are the most stubborn agricultural product, they are also one of the most esteemed. The tomato simply refuses to submit to our human efforts to bend it to our will, and thus a well-grown tomato bursting with its full flavor remains evocative of its season like few other fruits or vegetables. A taste of a tomato is like a taste of summer itself; its aroma and the scent of its leaves evoke warm days and golden sunlight. Even if we succeed in creating great-tasting tomatoes in, say, January, I question how right they will be when so far removed from their natural time. A tomato *belongs* to summer, and I say let's leave it there and preserve what we can in our freezers, dehydrators, and canning kettles to warm us through the winter months.

II

I called my friend Jerry the other evening. "What's happenin'?" I asked as I stirred onions and garlic simmering in olive oil. The smell was wonderful, provocative and ripe with promise.

"Making spaghetti" was the reply.

"The regular kind," I asked, "with onions and garlic and tomatoes?"

"That's the one," Jerry said, as I opened my can of crushed tomatoes and emptied it into the skillet.

A big pot of water was already boiling on the stove and a half pound of dry Italian spaghettini was sitting nearby. I'd sent my daughter Nicolle out to the garden to pick a little fresh oregano, and a chunk of Parmigiano Reggiano rested on the cutting board.

Now, Jerry and I are very different kinds of cooks. I've had dinner at his house that has included a salad with dozens of miniature marshmallows. He sometimes introduces me to friends, saying, "Hey, this is Michele. She had us to dinner and gave us vinegar ice cream for dessert." He laughs, and I keep quiet about marshmallows.

But over pots of spaghetti in our respective kitchens, our culinary paths intersect. I've never tasted Jerry's spaghetti, but I'll bet it's not all that different from mine. Strands of good semolina pasta cloaked in a mildly tart tomato sauce—what could be simpler, friendlier, more soothing and delicious? It is, for me anyway, the ultimate comfort food, better than cinnamon toast, more consoling than soup, infinitely yummier than anything made with chocolate.

I have eaten spaghetti at pivotal moments in my life and have sought solace in the simple preparation it requires. I have eaten spaghetti everywhere, at all times, and from as early as I can remember. I have eaten it at 4:00 A.M. in the hopes that it might prevent a hangover (it helps). I have eaten it in some of San Francisco's most expensive Italian restaurants, even though I knew I could have it at home the next day. I ate spaghetti in elementary school, from a wide-mouthed thermos when my mother finally caved in to my refusal to eat sandwiches. There have been times when I couldn't have it, like a long summer spent in India, when I ached with longing for the comfort it and nothing else provides.

A bite of spaghetti, or simply the sight of it, can trigger endless memories: spaghetti dinners on Halloween when my mother knew it was the one thing she could get me to eat; the time I first saw the Pacific Ocean on a school field trip and there was hot spaghetti waiting for me when I got home. On countless occasions in front of every refrigerator I've had, I have eaten it with my fingers, cold, doused with Tabasco sauce and extra salt. I have stood in the refrigerator's ghostly light, gathered up a few gooey strands with my fingers, held my hand high above my head and lowered the spaghetti into my mouth, letting its evocative power nourish my heart just as the sauce-covered noodles nourished my body.

III

"Hurry," I said to myself over and over in the spring of 1994 until the repetition sounded nearly like an incantation. *Hurry.* I was impatient, eager, I thought, to be done with this book and onto something else. As I finished a final edit of the manuscript, I realized that my impatience had not been with the book at all. It wasn't so much completion that I sought, though my deadline was a very real thing. What I really wanted was for the season itself to hurry up, for the mild days of spring to give way to the heat of summer. Simply, I wanted a tomato. I longed for one with growing pensiveness, but as luck would have it, it was a cool spring and thus a slow harvest. The wait seemed interminable. I checked my plants daily, but the little globes remained hard and green. How difficult it was to detail a tomato's delightful qualities without having them readily at hand as I wrote.

Finally, as I tended to the last details, the first tomato in my garden turned a luxurious red; a second blushed a warm and rich yellow, and then a third and a fourth, and the season was under way. Suddenly, as happens every year just about the time I think I'll burst with longing, wonderful tomatoes were everywhere. I set aside the wintery sauces, soups, and stews I'd been making with last year's harvest—so welcome in January, so dull by June—and began my yearly indulgence in gooey tomato sandwiches slathered with mayonnaise; delicate sliced tomatoes drizzled with luscious olive oil, topped with sweet red onions, creamy mozzarella cheese, silvery sardines. I called my friend Ginny and invited her over for savory tomato pie, still fragrant and warm from the oven. On the warmest days, I stayed cool with bowls of gazpacho. There was always plenty of fresh salsa.

For just three months—a little more if we're lucky—tomatoes are in such glorious abundance. I eat them every day, trying to get my fill before the first frost. Of course, I never succeed, and as the last of the year's tomatoes turn mushy after the first frost, the longing begins all over again, even as their taste lingers on my tongue. And so this book, the third in *The Good Cook's* series, is both an invocation and an invitation. Understand the nature of the tomato as a seasonal creature. Celebrate it, but as the days grow cold and the true tomato disappears, shun the substitutes that appear in the marketplace. Look instead to your pantry shelves and preserved tomatoes, and let the fire of longing build until, finally, there it will be next summer, and the summer after, the true tomato, tasting all the better because we've had to wait so long.

PART ONE

All About Tomatoes

CAN ANYONE DENY THE COMPELLING PLEASURE OF a summer tomato plucked right off the vine, still warm from the sun, eaten right there in the garden? Oblivious to spurts of seeds and dripping juices, we are at one with nature as we devour our succulent morsel. Has anything ever tasted better?

Every eager eater has his or her own variation of this tomato story, a memory of a pivotal sensual encounter. Many a crusade has begun this way, in gardens and farm stands, over backyard fences, in markets in the south of France. We recognize a true tomato with our first bite, and we seek a second with the fervor of a knight after the Holy Grail. The true tomato, that is what we crave, and once we have savored it we do not live well without it.

There is a broad, even enthusiastic, consensus about

what constitutes an authentically good tomato. The ideal tomato is heavy in the hand and has a pleasing, pungent aroma when we nuzzle close to it. It is encased in a thin skin that comes off easily should we decide to peel it (see sidebar, page 44). Should we cut it instead, it yields willingly beneath a sharp blade, without pressure or sawing. Once it is sliced, its flesh shines while small seed pockets glisten with thick gel. It feels silky to the tongue and its taste is both sweet and sharply acidic. Our tomato is entirely pleasing and satisfying, though we can devour it—and a few of its comrades as well—and not feel uncomfortably full. Our tomato offers pure, simple, sensual pleasure and gastronomic satisfaction. For the majority of people in the United States, it has become astonishingly hard to come by. Consumers' single greatest culinary lament is over the difficulty of finding good tomatoes, tomatoes "like they used to taste," tomatoes of what is generally called backyard quality.

There is little disagreement as to how to achieve a tomato of perfection. Follow a few elementary rules, and it is easy to end up with a daunting abundance of great tomatoes, much to the neighbors' delight. Articles and essays that praise the tomato do so in remarkably similar ways, evoking the pleasures of devouring the silky pulp in simple ways that accent the tomato's natural goodness. The suggestions of how and where and when to grow the best tomatoes are virtually the same as well, with subtle variations of variety, location, and method of cultivation, with specialized techniques developed by scores of award-winning home gardeners. But everyone agrees on the basic concept: Tomatoes should be grown for flavor; they must ripen on their vines; they should be eaten soon after picking; and they must not be refrigerated. It is an uncomplicated equation and backyard gardeners achieve success with ease and satisfaction.

Why then, has a good tomato been so hard to come by in a store? The demands of commercial farming—of getting the perishable little thing to the store, selling it at a price consumers will pay, and turning a profit—have diminished the pleasure the tomato once offered. For decades now, scientists and farmers have been relentlessly experimenting with tomatoes, seeking ways to deliver backyard flavor to the marketplace. Success has been limited, in spite of the ultimately simple solution to the dilemma: *Let the tomatoes ripen on the vine.*

No one praises standard commercial tomatoes—thick-skinned, cottony lumps that are picked green and never really ripen but simply turn red with the application of ethylene gas. The abuse is increased, not that it makes much difference, during refrigerated transportation and cold storage in both warehouses and markets, which halts the ripening process, renders the flesh mealy, and lowers the vitamin content. The result is appalling, an insult to both the fruit itself and the person eating it. Although farm markets are increasingly available in all parts of the country, offering beautiful, flavorful tomatoes in season, the majority of Americans still rely on major markets for most of their shopping. Nearly every supermarket in the country features mounds of these pale, mushy tomatoes whose taste bears not even a shadowy resemblance to what we seek. Why, then, do they continue to sell in such numbers? Are those of us with taste buds that recall the tomato's true pleasure really in such small numbers? Is it impatience, our distance from the seasons, our refusal to accept the fresh tomato as a seasonal creature, that make us demand it in January just as we crave it in July? Is it economics, as many farmers claim, that makes us refuse to pay the higher cost of getting good tomatoes to market? Everyone complains, but still those suspect tomatoes continue to sell. The commercial tomato market racks up an annual sales figure of about $4 billion, despite about a 30 percent drop-off in sales during the winter.

How did this happen? How did we get to this sorry state of inferior abundance and scarce quality? Will it change? What can we do? To find answers, it is helpful to know our tomato's history.

WHAT IS A TOMATO?

A tomato is the fruit of the tomato plant, a vine that in its wild state is robust and hearty, a resilient perennial that can grow as tall as a telephone pole or as wide as a row of Cadillacs and has an indefinite life span. Because the tomato develops from an ovary, it is, scientifically speaking, a fruit, although we think of it as a vegetable, which is how it functions on our table—in salads, soups, and main courses, in savory sauces and side dishes. Only occasionally, and with very limited success, does the tomato turn up in desserts. Thus it is functionally a vegetable, and legally, too, as the Supreme Court affirmed in a well-known 1893 decision (see sidebar).

The tomato plant is a member of the nightshade, or Solanaceae, family, making it a cousin of the eggplant, the

FRUIT OR VEGETABLE? *"Botanically speaking,"* wrote *Supreme Court Associate Justice Horace Gray for the majority in 1893, "tomatoes are the fruit of a vine, just as are cucumbers, squashes, beans, and peas. But in the common language of the people, whether sellers or consumers of provisions, all these are vegetables which are grown in kitchen gardens, and which, whether eaten cooked or raw, are, like potatoes, carrots, parsnips, turnips, beets, cauliflower, cabbage, celery, and lettuce, usually served at dinner in, with, or after the soup, fish, or meat which constitute the principal part of the repast, and not, like fruits generally, as dessert."*

The dispute arose because of a tariff imposed at the Port of New York, where a U.S. Customs agent deemed the red globes to be vegetables in spite of the importer's claim that the West Indian tomatoes were fruit. Vegetables were subject to a 10 percent tariff; fruits were duty-free. U.S. Customs prevailed, as revealed by Justice Gray's decision.

red pepper, the potato, the ground cherry, the tomatillo, and the highly toxic belladonna, also known as deadly nightshade. All tomatoes belong to the genus *Lycopersicon,* meaning "wolf peach," and those that we eat are limited, with a few exceptions, to cultivars of one species, *L. esculentum;* the tiny currant tomato, increasingly popular these days, belongs to the species *L. pimpellifolium.* The wild cherry tomato, the most likely ancestor of our cultivated tomatoes, is *L. esculentum* var. *cerasiforme,* cultivars of which are grown on a very limited basis.

The fruits of the tomato plant grow in a variety of

shapes, but each is made up of smooth, satiny skin surrounding meaty flesh that softens as the tomato ripens, with pockets known as locules filled with seeds surrounded by a thick gel. A well-grown tomato is always tart and always sweet, both in varying degrees, depending on the specific variety, climate, method of cultivation, and time of harvest. Tomatoes that are left to ripen on the vine have a higher percentage of sugar than do those that are picked green, which fail to develop their full flavor.

Although tomatoes vary greatly in appearance, their actual genetic differences are minute, attributable to a very limited number of genes. On a molecular level, all cultivated tomatoes are remarkably alike. Most of the differences in taste can be attributed to techniques of growing, though certain varieties have individual, if subtle, characteristics.

For general culinary purposes, the primary distinctions between tomatoes are size, color, and texture, with each category better suited to certain types of culinary uses than others. Currant tomatoes, tiny little jewels that are either red or yellow, are best eaten right off the vine or used as garnish. Cherry tomatoes—which come in a wide spectrum of colors from white, pink, and pale yellow to bright orange and deep red—are best raw in salads and salsas, grilled on skewers, or cooked simply as a side dish. Certain varieties of cherry tomatoes—the larger ones that have a low percentage of water—make delicious dried tomatoes. Plum tomatoes, with several varieties in various colors, are well suited for sauces, soups, stews, jams, and chutneys, and, because of their dense flesh, for drying. Slicing tomatoes include everything from the intensely flavored stupice, about two to two and a half inches in diameter, to the often enormous beefsteak and oxheart tomatoes, heirloom varieties currently enjoying a renaissance of popularity. Though ideal for their stated purpose, slicing, they also play their part in salsas, sauces, and soups quite well, although they frequently need draining or longer cooking because of their high water content. As specialty growers revive heirloom varieties—obtained through specialty seed catalogs—tomatoes with unique characteristics are becoming available, like the Valencia, a deep-orange slicer that holds its shape when it is cooked, and the yellow ruffle, a nearly hollow tomato that doesn't offer much taste but is ideal for stuffing. The increasingly available Green Grape cherry tomato, green when ripe, is delicious. Unlike their earliest relatives, which were largely ignored or shunned as food, tomatoes today have endless, delicious uses.

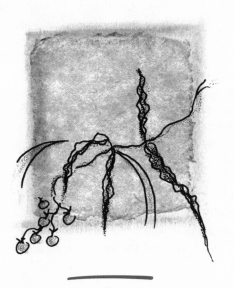

THE FIRST TOMATO

The tomato is a native of the New World, specifically of the South American tropics. Sometime long ago in a fertile river valley in the region now claimed primarily by Peru and Bolivia, a low green vine stretched itself out over the arid land, tumbled over rocks, wove itself between tree and shrub, and reached downward toward the sea. Flowers bloomed on our inaugural vine and gave way to tiny green berrylike fruit, the first tomatoes. Perhaps that primordial fruit was plucked off by an early ancestor; more likely, it shriveled on the vine until its dry skin burst and its seeds scattered on the hot wind.

Today, the progeny of that first tomato plant thrive throughout the Andean region, and some survive under extremely harsh conditions, pushing themselves up like weeds, which they were once considered, through cracks in concrete and frequently thriving with little water in near desertlike conditions. Human encroachment has had little impact. The tomato has staying power, as its lengthy struggle for culinary acceptance reveals.

The original ancestors had primarily green fruit—only three wild species show any color—whose size ranged from that of a small pea to that of today's cherry tomato, which is a direct descendant of the fruit of those early types. Although the wild species are not toxic—birds and animals feed on them—their complex taste, according to tomato geneticist Professor Charles Rick, is extremely distasteful to most people. Some have a high sugar content, but the flavors are unpleasant and persist in the mouth.

All wild species of the genus *Lycopersicon* can be traced

to the Andean region, yet there is no archeological evidence to suggest that the tomato was widely used as a food or that it was domesticated by the native inhabitants. There is no word for the tomato in the languages of the region, no images of them and no preserved remains, as is the case with other plants that were used as food. Further, there is no evidence of native large-fruited varieties, which were the first to appear in Europe. For clues about the tomato's early cultivation, we must look to Mexico.

THE TOMATO'S EARLY JOURNEY

In an article in *Scientific American*, Charles Rick explains that there is greater similarity between older European cultivars of tomatoes and the wild plants of Mexico than between the European varieties and wildlings of the Andean region. Woodcuts in early European herbals show large-fruited tomato plants, further strengthening the case for domestication before arrival in the Old World.

Unfortunately, early records of the New World rarely mention the tomato, making the story of the tomato's initial journey ultimately conjecture, based on inference rather than hard fact. However, we do know the source of its modern name. *Xitomatl*, the undisputed origin of *tomato*, is from Nahuatl, the language of the Nahua, a group of Mexican and other Central American Indian tribes, including the Aztecs. The tomato had to have moved north to be so named.

The timing is right, too. Cortés took Mexico City in 1519. The tomato makes its first appearance of record, though not by name, in 1544 in an herbal written by Petrus

Andreas Matthiolus of Italy, who also reports that the tomato "is eaten in Italy with oil, salt and pepper." Enough
time is thus allowed for Atlantic transport from Mexico,
European cultivation, and acceptance as food. Regardless of
this initial, simple appreciation, it would take several more
centuries before the tomato claimed its rightful place as an
indispensable element of the kitchen.

Although the first mention of the tomato is in an Italian publication, there is considerable evidence that it arrived in Europe by way of Seville, Spain, which dominated
New World trade in the sixteenth century. The Spanish
adopted the Nahuatl name, calling the fruit *tomate*, but the
tomato did not enjoy immediate popularity in the country.
The first published Spanish recipe (see sidebar, page 11)
appears in the seventeenth century, after both the Italian
reference and a full chapter in a 1554 publication by Dutch-
man Rembert Dodoens.

The tomato's name has generated substantial specula-
tion, and it is frequently assumed that the Italian designation is derived from *pomo d'oro*, or golden apple, which
would indicate that the first imported tomato seeds produced yellow fruit. However, in an essay in the *Journal of
Gastronomy*, the late Rudolf Grewe, a culinary historian, sug-
gests an alternative explanation involving the eggplant, a
close relative of the tomato. Popular among Arabs, the eggplant, Grewe speculates, became known as "apple of the
Moors," or *pomo del moro* in Italian and *pomme des mours* in
French. Both terms easily could have been shortened collo-
quially to *pomodoro* and *pomme d'amour*. Because of their bio-
logical similaries, described in the Matthiolus herbal in
1544, it is not far-fetched to imagine early tomatoes being

thought of as varieties of eggplant, and the name thus bestowed on the new fruit. This would explain, Grewe continues, the genesis of both the French and the Italian term, providing a plausible reason that the tomato became known in France as "the apple of love."

TOMATO SAUCE, SPANISH STYLE *Take half a dozen tomatoes that are ripe, and put them to roast in the embers, and when they are scorched, remove the skin diligently, and mince them finely with a knife. Add onions, minced finely, to discretion; hot chili peppers, also minced finely; and thyme in a small amount. After mixing everything together, adjust it with a little salt, oil, and vinegar. It is a very tasty sauce, both for boiled dishes or anything else.*

Antonio Latini, *Lo scalco alla moderna,*
vol. 1 (1692), trans. Rudolf Grewe

THE LOVE APPLE MAKES ITS MARK

From today's vantage point of the phenomenal popularity of tomatoes, it is hard to understand why it was so slow to capture the world's culinary imagination. But slow it was. Today, tomatoes are so abundant that their use gives new meaning to the name *Red Sea*. Just consider how much sauce is spread on pizza skins in a single year in the United States. A red sea, indeed, and that's just one use. Currently, the

United States alone produces fourteen to fifteen million tons of tomatoes each year. What took so long?

Although the tomato was eaten in Italy in the mid-1500s, it would be another couple of centuries before it secured its place in cuisines of the southern Mediterranean, where it remains essential today. Elsewhere throughout Europe, it would take even longer, and the tomato had to be reintroduced to the New World by Europeans—Puritans, no less, who brought it in as an ornamental plant—for the United States to become interested.

A statement by herbalist Matthias de L'Obel in 1581 was typical of the early difficulty experienced by the tomato: "These apples were eaten by some Italians like melons, but the strong stinking smell gives one sufficient notice how unhealthful and evil they are to eat." Malignant and poisonous, it was said, with no benefits for human nutrition.

Initially, the tomato was grown largely as an ornamental, its edible fruit treated with frivolous disregard. Myths about its pernicious and indeed deadly qualities persisted with great tenacity. Certainly, its relationship to poisonous members of the nightshade family didn't help, and perhaps that is the reason it was thought to be toxic. The tomato was approached timidly, with suspicion and uncertainty. If it wasn't poisonous, as surely must have been discovered—if not widely believed—fairly early, then it was an aphrodiasiac, an attribute perhaps linked to its name and one that would overshadow its culinary benefits, for better and for worse.

Before its fruit became a popular food, the tomato plant was examined for any possible medicinal effects, and it was found that an alkaloid, tomatine, present primarily in the leaves, was beneficial in treating fungal diseases of the skin. Plants high in this alkaloid show resistance to fungi, an immunity that apparently can be passed on. It was also considered effective against scabies and arthritis, benefits that have not been confirmed in modern times. In fact, consumption of members of the nightshade family can make the symptoms of arthritis worse.

The tomato makes its first written appearance in the United States in an herbal published in 1710, a full 72 years before Thomas Jefferson makes the next reference to it. Always the sophisticate when it came to things culinary, Jefferson continues to acknowledge both the horticultural and culinary possibilities of "tomatas" in the Monticello garden book that he maintained from 1809 to 1814.

Clearly, by the nineteenth century tomatoes were gaining wide acceptance and limited but increasing appreciation. They were being grown as a food crop, and their name began appearing in association with ketchup, traditionally made with such ingredients as walnuts and mushrooms. By the 1850s numerous varieties of tomato plants were available from seed salesmen.

Although the tomato continued to be scorned in publications such as the *Boston Globe* as late as 1845, by 1847 Robert Buist in *The Family Kitchen Gardener* claimed that "it is on every table from July to October." Also that year the commercial processing of tomatoes began at Lafayette College in Easton, Pennsylvania. It was the chief gardener at the college, Harrison Woodhull Crosby, who spawned the tomato canning industry. He soldered lids on tin pails, leaving a hole on top into which he stuffed whole tomatoes. Next, he soldered a small tin plate over the hole, and then sterilized the tins in boiling water. By 1914, the tomato processing industry was enjoying great success, with thousands of bushels of tomatoes used to produce not only simple canned tomatoes, but soups, ketchup, and chili sauce as well.

In 1994 the Campbell Soup Company celebrated its 125th anniversary. It was the tomato that got this company started in 1869 in Camden, New Jersey. The famous—some would say, infamous—Campbell's Condensed Tomato Soup spawned an industry, and by 1990 the company had produced 20 billion cans of it. Today, Campbell's remains committed to tomato research and improvement. Currently, its focus is largely on the nutritional possibilities of the golden tomato. Golden tomatoes are higher in beta-carotene (see page 15) than red ones, and new golden varieties may eventually contain 100 percent of the recommended intake of vitamin A.

Along the way from scorn and obscurity to praise and prominence, the tomato has had its heroes, both real and mythical. Tomato folklore includes the largely fictional account of Robert Gibbon Johnson, who is said to have eaten a tomato—allegedly, the first consumed in this country—on the steps of the courthouse in Salem, New Jersey, in August 1820, thus promoting the safety of the fruit. A look into the actual history of the tomato, the town, and the man does not support this fanciful tale of the tomato in America, but it is a good story. An Ohio seed salesman, Alexander W. Livingston (1821–98), is honored in the annual Reynoldsburg Tomato Festival, founded in 1973, for his efforts in dispelling the myth of tomatoes as poisonous. And today, of course, there are scientists like the esteemed Charles Rick, who is known casually as Mr. Tomato, a high compliment in today's world.

MR. TOMATO: A PORTRAIT OF CHARLEY
RICK, THE FATHER OF TOMATO GENETICS

*Several months out of the year, the tomato makes up about 50
percent of Professor Charles Rick's diet. His favorite recipe is
simple enough: He makes a sandwich using toasted heavy bread,
mayonnaise, tomato slices, basil vinegar, salt, and pepper. "I eat
it all the time and never get tired of it," he says, an illustrative
answer to my inquiry about how he feels about eating tomatoes
after five decades of studying them. Not only does he eat tomatoes with enthusiasm, he grows them in his backyard and makes
his own dried tomatoes, using a Cuisinart for slicing and a
forced-air dehydrator with temperature control.*

*Rick, professor emeritus in the Vegetable Crops Department at
the University of California at Davis, has devoted his entire
professional life to the study of tomatoes, and he remains an un-
fettered enthusiast. As a young faculty member in 1940, he
didn't start out with a passionate interest in* Lycopersicon, *but
rather spent his first years studying the asparagus, with an em-
phasis on gender determination. One day after he'd been on the
faculty a couple of years, an older professor commented that it
might be interesting to look at a common phenomenon out in the
tomato fields: about one plant in a thousand failed to set fruit.
Rick thought it sounded boring and initially dismissed the sug-
gestion, saying to himself, "Better to know why they set fruit."*

*He remembers that about a month later he woke up in a cold
sweat, thinking, "You fool, you'd better look at this." Awake the
rest of the night, he spent the next day gathering field samples*

and the remainder of the season studying the fruitlessness of certain tomato plants. He uncovered a multitude of fascinating details, information that led to years of study and a remarkable body of knowledge.

The discoveries Rick made that season proved to be extremely useful, not just in studying the tomato and eventually developing improved varieties, but in mapping the genome as well. The chromosomal maps of the tomato are among the best of any flowering plant. By the 1950s, Rick was aware of the wild relatives of the contemporary cultivated tomato, and he began spending his sabbaticals in the Andes, collecting specimens and studying habitat. It was this crucial research that was partly responsible for the vast number of disease-resistant varieties available to growers, both commercial and casual, today.

Now in his fifth decade at UC-Davis, Charley Rick oversees the Tomato Genetics Resource Center, which catalogs and stores the seeds of about 3,000 types of tomato plants, including around 1,000 wild species, subspecies, and varieties. Each year it is necessary to replenish the library seed stock of about 300 varieties, a project Rick also administers.

GROWING TOMATOES

Because tomatoes are easy to grow and because those from home gardens almost always taste better than those grown anywhere else at all, a tremendous amount of support and information is available to the home gardener, the result of all of the research, experience, knowledge, and enthusiasm that has accumulated for decades (see Resources and Bibliography, pages 291–296). There exists an entire subculture of backyard tomato growers who pursue their passion with great gusto and dedication and who make their considerable knowledge easily available to aficionados. Whether it is recommendations for seeds for hundreds of varieties with every imaginable characteristic or solutions to every problem from a short growing season to soil nematodes, information abounds that will get you from cultivation of a garden patch to bushels of great tomatoes without much trouble. Growing great tomatoes in your backyard is largely a matter of a few simple techniques and a lot of trial and error as you determine which varieties work best in your particular environment and what, if any, special considerations might be needed.

It is important to understand the basic requirements of the tomato plant before setting out to grow one. Although not temperamental, the plant has specific needs, with different varieties being better suited to certain environments. Tomatoes require at least eight hours of sunlight a day, so if you live in a northern area where the season is short, consider one of the early-fruiting varieties. There are several, from the well-known Early Girl to numerous heirloom varieties. If you have only a tiny spot on a fire escape in Manhattan, you can get varieties ideal for container cultivation. Temperatures under 50 degrees for more than the briefest periods will damage both fruit and plant, so again, consider your environment before planting. A company in Northern California offers individual solar green houses, small plastic tents that are filled with water, that enable growers in cooler climates to start their tomato plants several weeks earlier than normal, but if cold nights linger into June, you need to choose varieties with the shortest production time.

Tomatoes don't do well in sustained temperatures much over 90 degrees, though they thrive on heat, and an occasional sizzler won't hurt them. But in areas with particularly hot summers, such as southern Florida, it is impossible to grow good tomatoes during the summer months. Likewise, tomatoes do not do well in high humidity. The plants become prey to all sorts of fungal diseases and nearly always need to be treated with fungicides. Certain varieties have been developed to set fruit in cooler weather, such as the San Francisco fog, and these varieties are said to do better in hotter weather, too. Basically, it appears their temperature tolerance has been stretched in both directions.

Tomatoes need a proper chemical balance in the soil, with nitrogen available in moderate but not abundant amounts. Too much nitrogen and you will have bushy tomato trees without fruit; too little, and the fruit will be puny. In addition to nitrogen, tomato plants need a mix of phosphorus, potassium, sulfur, calcium, magnesium, iron, zinc, molybdenum, manganese, boron, and chlorine. The most efficient way to ensure that all of these minerals are available to your plants is by using good compost or organic fertilizers such as bat guano and blood meal. Should deficient soil be your problem, consult an expert on how to nourish it.

Tomatoes can become easily waterlogged and require good drainage. Careful watering techniques are crucial; too much or too little water causes a plant a great deal of stress. Certainly, plants must be irrigated in dry weather, but in optimum conditions, water can be withheld entirely during the last stages of maturity. Tomatoes that are watered appropriately have better texture and more intense flavor than their overwatered relatives.

Because diseases can pose a severe problem, several experts recommend growing varieties that have had resistance, especially to the common VFN (verticillium wilt, fusarium wilt, and soil nemotodes), bred into them. Nonresistant heirloom varieties are somewhat trickier to grow, but many gardeners find the gamble worth it; the harvest is diverse, colorful, unusual, and delicious. Nearly all seed packages will state whether a variety has VFN resistance or not.

The best way to find great tomatoes, if in fact you can't grow them, is to spot them in your neighbor's yard or to have a friend nearby who grows them, so be on the lookout. Of course, if that is not possible, look for the best commercial sources, especially the farm markets now available in most urban as well as suburban areas.

VARIETIES OF TOMATOES

You hear a lot about tomato varieties these days. Heirloom tomatoes have become extremely fashionable and are available not just to industrious gardeners but to eager eaters who frequent farm markets. Restaurants, too, are in on the designer-tomato trend; many buy specialty tomatoes directly from the farmers. This is a real boon to tomato lovers, who have a greater variety available to them currently than they have had in several decades.

With a few notable exceptions, we generally do not know the names of the tomatoes we buy. Although everyone talks about varieties of tomato by name, the vast majority of tomatoes, certainly nearly all commercial stock, are not named at all, but instead identified by numbers. A farmer wanting to grow a tomato with certain qualities can contact the University of California at Davis and choose from thousands of varieties. These tomatoes make their way into cans and onto produce shelves without ever being identified by such charming names as their heirloom cousins sport, such as Charlie's Pride & Joy, Super Sioux, Heart-shaped Brandywine, and Egyptian Tomb, to mention just a few. A handful of named varieties have made their way into our common vernacular and we find them easily in seed packets, in six-packs of tomato starts at our local nursery, or in the produce bins of a few good markets. The most common of these are Sweet 100, Early Girl, Celebrity, Better Boy, Best Boy, Roma, Red Currant, Yellow Taxi, Yellow Pear, Green Grape, Zebra Stripe, and Marvel Stripe.

If you are intrigued by the prospect of growing heirloom tomatoes, several resources are available to you. One of the best is Seed Savers Exchange in Decorah, Iowa. This seed-preservation organization publishes an annual yearbook with thousands of listings of varieties of plants from apples, barley, beans, and corn to flax, millet, onions, and tomatoes. Each variety listed is grown by at least one member of Seed Savers Exchange; a few seeds are available directly from that member for a small fee. Descriptions of each variety list qualities—good and bad—and occasionally historical trivia as well. The book not only offers an enormous amount of information, but is filled with a great deal of charm, too.

TOMATO CULTIVARS FOR GARDENS AND SMALL FARMS

This is a sampling of a few of the thousands of tomato varieties available to home gardeners and small farmers. (The type designation—currant, cherry, paste, slicer, beefsteak, and stuffer—refers to the size, shape, or texture of the tomato and should not be confused with varieties of the same or similar names.)

VARIETY	TYPE	CHARACTERISTICS	BEST USES
Ruby Pearl	Red currant	Tiny, very sweet	Garnishes; salads
Broad Ripple Yellow	Yellow currant	True currant, early to ripen, prolific; very sweet, dime-sized fruit	Garnishes; salads
Sweet 100	Red cherry	Hybrid; intensely sweet and juicy; abundant yield	Salads; salsas; grilling
Sun Gold	Orange cherry	Richly colored with intense, distinctive flavor	Salads; salsas; grilling; drying

VARIETY	TYPE	CHARACTERISTICS	BEST USES
Green Grape	Green cherry	Large, with lots of flavor and good strong acid	Salads; salsas and other fresh sauces
Pink Teardrop	Pink cherry	Pale pink, with a musky flavor	Salads; salsas and other fresh sauces
Camp Joy	Red cherry	Size of a Ping-Pong ball; excellent flavor	Drying
Yellow Pear	Yellow cherry	Beautiful, yellow, pear-shaped; sweet	Salads; salsas
Snow white	Yellow cherry	Ruffled, pale yellow with white interior; musky flavor	Salads; salsas; delicate sauces
Tiger Tom	Striped cherry	Red fruit with golden stripes; size of golf ball; very tasty	Salads; salsas and other fresh sauces
Roma	Red paste	Good flavor, high yield, meaty; best canning tomato	Canning; sauces; ketchup; drying
San Marzano	Red paste	Meaty, mild	Canning; sauces; ketchup; drying
Orange Roma	Orange paste	Brightly colored, mild-tasting fruit; low acid	Canning; sauces; ketchup; drying
Yellow Plum	Yellow paste	Meaty fruit, good sweet flavor; prolific	Sauces; jams; ketch-up; slicing; salads
Rocky	Red paste	Red fruit with fan-tastic flavor; sweet and meaty	Slicing; canning; sauces; ketchup; drying
Enchantment	Red paste	Egg-shaped; wonder-ful fresh taste	Slicing; canning; sauces; drying

VARIETY	TYPE	CHARACTERISTICS	BEST USES
Banana Legs	Yellow paste	Shaped like a Roma with a bump on the end; mushy; poor flavor	Novelty appearance is only appeal
Early Girl	Red slicer	Very popular early tomato; small, great true tomato taste	Salads, sandwiches, salsas and other fresh sauces; roasting
Stupice	Red slicer	Small red with outstanding flavor; fine in heat but adapts to cool climates with short seasons	Salads, sandwiches, salsas and other fresh sauces; roasting
Dona	Red slicer	French hybrid, easy and reliable to grow; great, true tomato flavor	Salads, sandwiches; salsas and other fresh sauces; roasting
San Francisco Fog	Red slicer	Medium red with good temperature tolerance & good taste	Sandwiches, salsas and other fresh sauces
Valencia	Orange slicer	Firm orange flesh, few seeds; retains shape when cooked; can be difficult to grow	Stir-fry; chutneys; salsas and other fresh sauces
Peach	Yellow slicer	Pale yellow fruit with an apricot blush; fuzzy; delicate, subtle flavor	Slicing, salads, sandwiches
Taxi	Yellow slicer	Medium-sized bright yellow fruit; wonderful, old-fashioned flavor	Slicing, salads, sandwiches; salsas and other fresh sauces
Great White	White slicer	Slight melon flavor	Delicate sauces such as vinaigrettes; salads

VARIETY	TYPE	CHARACTERISTICS	BEST USES
White Wonder	White slicer	Ivory-colored with a pale yellow blush; good taste	Delicate sauces such as vinaigrettes; salads
Green Zebra	Green slicer	Small tomato with yellowish stripes	Slicing, salsas and other fresh sauces
Red Rose	Red beefsteak	Large red fruit; great flavor; cross between Brandywine and Rutgers	Slicing; grilling; summer soups
Evergreen	Green beefsteak	Large; bright-green flesh; great flavor	Slicing; salads; gazpacho; salsas and other fresh sauces
Caro Rich	Orange beefsteak	Large deep-orange fruit, low in acid; high in beta carotene; sweet and mild	Gazpacho; slicing; salsas and other fresh sauces
Brandywine	Dark red beefsteak	Large; old-time tomato flavor	Gazpacho; slicing; salsas and other fresh sauces
Marvel Stripe	Marbled beefsteak	Flesh is marbled yellow and red; very large; full of good flavor	Slicing; salads; salsas and other fresh sauces
Black Krim	Dark beefsteak	Large Russian tomato, dark reddish brown or purple, green shoulders; unique, full-bodied flavor	Slicing; salads; sandwiches; grilling
Yellow Ruffle	Yellow stuffer	Nearly hollow yellow tomato with minimal flavor	Stuffing

Sources: Seed Savers Exchange; Johnny's Selected Seeds; Dragonfly Farms; Grand-view Farms.

In the days when we all lived closer to the land, it was common practice to pull up the last of the tomato plants—those still heavy with green fruit—by their roots and hang them, upside down, on the walls of the root cellar, pantry, or, in the proper climate, a protected back porch. The tomatoes would ripen slowly, stretching out the season for a few more precious weeks. There is no reason this can't be done today and I am sure it still is, though fewer of us have our own tomato plants, and even fewer have a root cellar or a pantry large enough to accommodate a bush or two on the wall. Should you be blessed with both land and space, give it a try, being sure to sort through the branches every few days

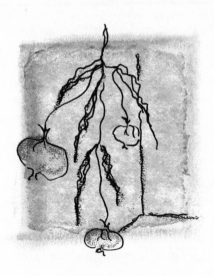

and pluck off not just the ripe fruit but any that may have spoiled. Plants hung in this fashion are particularly vulnerable to insects, and so you must pay close atttention to protect your bounty.

There are alternatives to this most romantic of tomato preservation techniques. If you have two or three days to set aside at the peak of harvest, you can make it through the winter with a pantry stocked with wonderful preserved tomatoes. If you have a garden, perhaps you already preserve the essence of the tomato season in jars, bottles, and freezer bags. But you don't have to grow your own tomatoes to take advantage of their season. At the height of the harvest, an abundance of tomatoes must be dealt with pronto, before the rotting process sets in. It's neither difficult nor expensive to purchase a few lugs of them to put up for the cooler months.

These days, you can even make your own dried tomatoes easily with a forced-air dehydrator. For cooking, the best tomatoes to dry with this handy machine are Romas, with their thick, meaty flesh and low percentage of water. For snacking, however, both cherry tomatoes and slicing tomatoes—cut very thin—are delightfully sweet and tangy. Dehydrators come with instructions for drying a variety of fruits and vegetables.

Tomatoes take well to freezing as long as they are sealed in airtight packages and used within about three months. Simply peel them, remove the stem end, and freeze them whole or coarsely chopped. Of course, frozen tomatoes cannot be used to replace fresh ones, but they are fine for soups and sauces. Most tomato sauces can be frozen, too; just pack them in conveniently sized containers.

Finally, putting up tomatoes—a somewhat more laborious task than drying or freezing—is a great way to spend a couple of days in the dead of summer (see Preserving Tomatoes, pages 279–285, for specific techniques and recipes). You might begin by reading about others who do it. *On Persephone's Island* by Mary Taylor Simetti includes a wonderfully evocative account of the long tradition of making tomato sauce in Sicily.

Making the year's supply of tomato sauce is the most important domestic ritual in the Sicilian summer, and each housewife believes in the efficacy of her favorite method with fervor equal to that with which she believes in the efficacy of her favorite saint. There are basically two rival schools of thought: the one favors passing the scalded tomatoes through the tomato mill, then sterilizing the filled and capped bottles in boiling water; the other prefers to heat up the empty bottles, fill them with boiling hot tomato sauce, and then lay them in a nest of woolen blankets, so well wrapped that they will take several days to cool off.

Mary Taylor Simetti, *On Persephone's Island*

COMMERCIAL TOMATOES

Today, California dominates the commercial tomato industry, with 90 percent of the nation's tomato crop coming from the Golden State, where the arid conditions most closely mirror the tomato's original environment. California's typical lack of rainfall from April through October is ideal for tomatoes, which suffer from too much moisture. Although California could produce outstanding tomatoes, and does so on a limited basis, the majority of the crop is tasteless—grown to bounce, as one detractor puts it. Seventy percent of tomatoes for fresh sales are picked at the mature green stage, well before the natural sugars and acids have had time to develop. They are reddened with the application of ethylene gas. "Vine-ripened" tomatoes, which represent 30 percent of the market, are picked at the breakers, or turning, stage and have only the barest hint of color. These tomatoes generally are left to ripen on their own, without being gassed, though their full flavors fail to develop once they are removed from the vine.

Although there are a number of specialty growers in the state who offer a great variety of true vine-ripened tomatoes, production is very low, forming barely a fraction of the commercial tomato industry. Still, good tomatoes are there to be had by the lucky or diligent shopper.

Even sunny California has an off-season, which spans from the first winter frost, generally sometime in October though occasionally as early as mid-September, until the beginning of the next year's harvest, during which time Florida and Mexico play important roles in the fresh tomato industry. Florida dominates the market, with Mexico frequently offering fierce competition. Florida production drops off as summer approaches; the temperatures are simply too high for the tomato to thrive. Fungal diseases are also a problem in Florida, where the high humidity encourages their growth. Nearly all Florida tomatoes are treated with fungicides.

Setting aside the consideration of taste just momentarily, the strides made by the tomato industry in the last several decades are astonishing. Yields have increased significantly as acreage devoted to commercial tomato production actually has decreased, owing largely to the pioneering work of Professor Charles Rick. Forty years ago, California's yield was approximately 13.5 metric tons of tomatoes per hectare; today it is over 50. Rick's research with the ancient wild tomatoes of the Andes has resulted in new varieties that are resistant to diseases capable of decimating entire crops and have opened up areas to cultivation where tomatoes once failed to thrive. The soil nematode, for example, made it impossible to grow tomatoes in certain soils until scientists developed a variety immune to the nematodes. But in spite of these advances, corporate agribusiness, both in California and elsewhere, faces numerous problems—from the overuse of chemical pesticides and fertilizers and lack of crop rotation to the mistreatment of migrant farmworkers and the cultivation of foods for maximum profit rather than for taste and nutritional value. These problems are best discussed elsewhere, but it is important to keep them in mind when considering the shortcomings of commercial tomatoes.

COMMERCIAL TOMATO PRODUCTS

Like tomatoes grown for general commercial distribution, tomatoes used to produce the many products on our shelves, from simple canned whole tomatoes to chili sauce, ketchup, soups, and stews, are from determinate vines, plants that produce their fruit all at the same time. This allows for mechanical harvesting and gets an entire field of tomatoes picked and to the processor quickly. Unlike tomatoes grown for fresh distribution, tomatoes for processing can and generally do remain on the vine until both their color and their flavor develop—they are usually picked at the light red stage, when their sugar and acid levels are high—which is the primary reason that canned tomatoes tend to be far superior, even in the summer months, to standard commercial tomatoes. In winter and spring, there is no comparison between canned tomato products and commercial fresh tomatoes. But that may be changing with the introduction of the genetically engineered tomato (see Tomatoes of the Future, page 34).

Several varieties of tomatoes are used for commercial canning and rarely is the variety named. Rather, it is chosen from among hundreds of numbered varieties, sought for specific qualities such as high sugar, low water, high yield, good flavor, and disease resistance. In addition, growers seek tomatoes with specific traits that allow them to thrive in particular soils and climates.

For many years, canned tomatoes imported from Italy were said to be far superior to domestic brands. These imports were generally known as San Marzano, a popular variety of Roma tomato named for a specific region near Naples that has traditionally grown them in great number, and the designation was enough to sell them over other brands, even though the name often specified simply San Marzano *style*. The reputation of San Marzano tomatoes remained steady through the mid-1980s, with noted cookbook authors and food editors indicating these tomatoes in their recipes. Several taste tests, including those whose results appear in *Cook's Illustrated* (March/April 1994) and Jennifer Harvey Lang's *Tasting*, reveal a reversal in this trend. Although *Cook's Illustrated* blames higher tariffs for the decline in Italian tomato products—the assumption being that it is no longer profitable to pack them for export—several importers offer another explanation. Certainly, the imposition of a 100 percent tariff on imported tomatoes makes them less attractive than their California equivalents, but the quality has decreased as well. Industrial pollution is a severe problem and areas that once produced vast quantities of high-quality tomatoes have been adversely affected, not only in their yield, but also in the quality of their product.

Currently, a few brands coming from Italy offer excellent-quality tomatoes, but it is no longer safe to assume that the choice of an import—which is usually two to three times more expensive than its domestic equivalent—ensures quality. I frequently use Pomi tomatoes, a brand distributed by Parmalat U.S.A. Corporation, which are packed in small boxes rather than cans. I find they offer dependable taste and texture. I also use the San Marzano tomatoes imported by Taste of the World (Morristown, New Jersey) when I can find them.

TIMBER CREST FARMS

Imagine a tomato field at midnight, cloaked not in a quiet cape of darkness but lit by bright halogen lamps and teeming with activity. Huge truck-trailers pull in to receive their loads of juicy red fruit and take off into the cover of night, winding their way to the heart of the wine country, to Dry Creek Valley in Healdsburg, California, where some of the state's finest zinfandel grapes are grown. Here you will also find Timber Crest Farms and its resident tomato visionary, Ruth Waltenspiel, the woman who single-handedly created the American dried-tomato industry. Every night through-

out California's tomato harvest, trucks snake their way from the north central valley toward this small town in northern Sonoma County so that at the crack of dawn the work can begin. The tomatoes are floated out of the trucks and trailers on a bath of cool, clean water. They go through several additional rinses before they are sorted, cut in half, set on racks, and wheeled into huge dryers, from which they will emerge a few hours later to again be sorted and sent on their way, either to storage or for additional processing as dried-tomato bits, dried tomatoes marinated in olive oil, or the other Sonoma brand dried-tomato products of Timber Crest Farms.

All this began in 1979, when Ruth Waltenspiel returned home from a gourmet-food show determined to compete with the high-priced sun-dried tomatoes imported from Italy and then just becoming popular among trendy eaters. She was allowed two truckloads. Processing went beautifully on the first load, and when at about 2:00 A.M. the tomatoes seemed to be drying beautifully, she turned off the heaters and the fans that had previously dried only the fruits that she and her husband produced. She went to bed. An early morning phone call brought the news of green mold, and that was the end of the first truckload of dried tomatoes, which ended up in the orchard as compost. The next truckload was more successful, and Timber Crest Farms was on its way to creating a domestic dried-tomato industry. In 1993 the farm processed 913 truck and trailer loads of tomatoes, or over seven million pounds of Roma tomatoes. Timber Crest Farms remains the leader in the industry.

TOMATOES OF THE FUTURE

There are two general trends in the commercial tomato market. The movement toward organic products is immensely important, and best represented currently by Muir Glen, a company based in Sacramento, California, that is producing high-quality tomato products from organically grown fruit. The other significant development comes to us from nearby, in the university town of Davis just south of Sacramento, where a snappy young biotech firm, Calgene, Inc., is working to place tomatoes with true backyard flavor into every supermarket in America.

Although Muir Glen is neither the first nor the only producer of organic canned tomatoes—Eden Foods launched its organic crushed tomatoes in 1990—its aggressive marketing plan and beautiful, bold packaging have brought dramatically increased awareness of the availability of organic tomato products. A division of the large Sierra Quality Canners, Muir Glen is producing canned whole tomatoes, ground tomatoes, diced tomatoes, tomato juice, tomato sauce, tomato paste, and several other tomato products from organically grown tomatoes. Founded in 1990, the company that was named in honor of the great nineteenth-century environmentalist John Muir has doubled its production each year.

Muir Glen contracts directly with organic farmers throughout California's Central Valley to grow tomatoes to its specifications. After harvest, the tomatoes are trucked to Sierra Quality Canners' facility in Gilroy for processing. Muir Glen's tomatoes are packed in lead-free steel containers that have been lined with white enamel to eliminate the slight metallic taste of many canned tomato products. Interestingly, in both casual and formal taste tests, many consumers have shown a preference for tomatoes that have picked up a bit of taste from the can, a fact that underscores the power of sensory memory. Many dishes based on canned tomatoes are comfort foods, things like the homemade spaghetti that we ate as children. If mama cooked with metallic-tasting tomatoes, that longing for the foods of youth will be satisfied by the same flavors, the faint taste of metal included. Increasingly, though, people are coming to realize the benefits—both to themselves and to the environment—of organic products. And those who make the switch to organic tomatoes without metallic residue will raise a generation who seek their unadulterated flavor.

The other trend in commercial tomato production involves fresh fruit and is basically a challenge to the tomato's perishable nature. In the natural world, tomatoes left on the vine until their flavor is fully developed have a short postharvest life, four or five days at most. That's plenty of time to get a crop of tomatoes to the processor for canning, but getting fresh tomatoes to the marketplace poses a much greater challenge. Calgene has been working since 1982 to develop a technique that will add time to a tomato's postharvest life, thus allowing it to ripen on the vine and still make it to markets far from the field. The company appears to have succeeded: in spring 1994 it won approval from the Food and Drug Administration for the new designer tomato. In early summer, the tomato was introduced in a few limited regions of California and Illinois, and initial sales were phenomenal, far beyond Calgene's projections.

The FlavrSavr, or MacGregor, tomato, as Calgene's creation has been named, is the first genetically engineered product to be offered for sale, and the process has sparked no small controversy. To grasp the issues, we must understand how the tomato has been created. A gene in all tomatoes triggers the production of an enzyme that degrades pectin, causing the tomatoes to soften, the initial stage in the process of rotting, which begins soon after ripe fruit is picked. Because ripe tomatoes are highly perishable, allowing little time for them to be picked, packed, shipped, unloaded, displayed, and sold to consumers all over the country, most tomatoes are picked at the mature green stage.

After identifying the gene that triggers the release of the pectin-hungry enzyme, Calgene scientists clone the gene, reverse it, and reinsert it into the tomato so that it gives a negative, or *antisense*, message. The process of pectin degradation is stalled and the life of a ripe tomato is extended by at least 14 days. At this point, the altered tomato contains only its own DNA—albeit altered, but its own nonetheless. Calgene has been issued a patent on this process, antisense RNA technology, that covers not just its function in the FlavrSavr tomato, but in a broad range of plants. The technology enables a partial or complete inhibition of specific plant functions.

In order to identify those plants that have undergone successful gene reversal—the insertion of the altered gene doesn't always work—a marker gene is attached to the side of the reversed gene. This marker gene, which comes from a naturally occurring bacterium, creates an immunity to kanamycin, the antibiotic present in the test medium in which Calgene's tomatoes are grown. The FlavrSavr seeds are resistant to the drug and thrive; those without the reversed gene, and thus without immunity, die or fail to thrive adequately. Calgene can therefore identify the FlavrSavr tomato without waiting for harvest and then setting tomatoes on a shelf and watching them rot.

What Calgene has bought with its high-tech engineering is time. The antisense gene allows the tomatoes to ripen on the vine and extends their postharvest life so that they can make it to markets around the country with time to spare. The specific function of the altered gene appears benign; it is the marker gene and its resistance to antibiotics that is the lightning rod for objections to the tomato, in spite of extensive testing that confirms its safety. Each tomato does contain the resistant marker gene—in miniscule quantitites of less than five ten-thousandths of a percent—though all tests indicate that there are no adverse effects—no increased immunity to antibiotics, for example.

Tim Hartz, head of vegetable crop production at UC-Davis, scoffs at most of the opponents of genetic engineering, comparing them to those who have resisted everything from Galileo's view of the solar system to the invention of the loom. But he is not a strong advocate of the designer tomato, regarding it as a high-tech solution to a problem that could be easily solved without advanced genetics. He sees some irony in the situation when he explains that vine-ripened tomatoes could be available 365 days a year. The reason they aren't is that consumers so far have been unwilling to pay the higher price they must command. Postharvest costs soar for vine-ripened fruit because they must be handled more carefully and get to market more quickly. Hartz suspects that once farmers see that consumers are willing to pay a premium price for the engineered tomato, they will be eager to compete for a share of the ripe-tomato market. He predicts the appearance of better-quality tomatoes in the major markets, a tomato war of sorts fought not only in lab petri dishes, but also in the fields of old-fashioned, low-tech farmers who may finally be able to engineer a profit out of vine-ripened tomatoes. This is extremely good news for tomato lovers.

TASTING THE FRUITS OF BIOTECHNOLOGY I *arrived at Calgene, Inc., early one morning and was led into an employees' lunchroom, where Carolyn Hayworth, manager of public relations, handed me a plump red MacGregor tomato with a blue, green, and red sticker over the stem end. The tomato was heavy in my hand; it was deeply colored and had a ripe feeling.* It is an attractive tomato, *I thought to myself, in spite of a few yellow blemishes Hayworth apologized for. The spots didn't bother me; in fact, they made me feel more comfortable.* It's real, I *thought as I turned it in my palm.* It is not a monster. *Of course, blemished fruit such as the one I held will be discarded before it gets to market. Customer resistance to such flaws is much higher than resistance to pesticides, herbicides, or genetic engineering. Interestingly, statistics show greater consumer concern about the safety of organic products than about that of genetically altered ones.*

I sliced the MacGregor tomato in half, noticing the pleasant way it yielded to the knife. It fell open to reveal deep red flesh, plenty of it, and small, tightly packed seed pockets. It glistened invitingly and a faint tomato aroma beckoned. It looked as though it would make a good gazpacho. Did I hesitate a moment before slicing off a piece? Was I wary of the marker gene, afraid I might be violating some natural sanctity of body that was hitherto pristine, untouched, a biogenetic virgin? Frankly, no, my brazenness stemming perhaps from the fact that I am a child of the '60s, a member of a generation with a long history of chemical experimentation. Why stop now?

I followed my first bite with a second, and then a third, considering flavor, texture, acidity, balance, and finish. I added a little salt to one bite, cut pieces in different shapes, and tried those. The tomato was slightly sweet and had a pleasantly silky texture, plenty of tomato flavor, and just a bit of characteristic acid. There was no getting around it; this was a damn good tomato, not the best I've ever tasted but far better than anything I've ever gotten in a supermarket.

I finished every last bit of my first MacGregor tomato and headed home, stopping at a nearby supermarket, where I picked out a tomato that sat under a "Garden Fresh" sign. The tomato was hard in my hand but not particularly heavy. It was the same pale pinkish red as all the other tomatoes in the large pile. I brought it home and cut into it; it didn't give under the knife at all. The inside flesh was hard and the seed pockets were large and full of runny liquid. There was no aroma. I sliced off a piece and tasted it. Tasteless, except for a sharp bite of acidity. If this, the supermarket tomato, is MacGregor's competition, I know where I'd place my bet.

Although, with one exception, a single tomato is not remarkably high in any particular nutrient, we eat such a substantial quantity—currently about 80 pounds per person annually—that they provide a larger percentage of dietary nutrients than any other fruit or vegetable. A tomato doesn't even make it into the top ten when it comes to nutrient concentration (the top spots go to broccoli, spinach, brussels sprouts, lima beans, peas, asparagus, artichokes, cauliflower, sweet potatoes, and carrots, in that order); the tomato comes in at 16, just after cabbage and before bananas, but we eat so many of them that they top the chart when it comes to their contribution to our diet. (Nutrient-rich broccoli, spinach, and brussels sprouts are 21, 18, and 34, respectively.)

A tomato is made up mostly of water (but so are we). The tomato's nutrients include vitamin A and a substantial amount of vitamin C (about 32 percent of the Recommended Dietary Allowance), trace amounts of several other vitamins, a bit of iron and other minerals, a little fiber, and a very small amount of protein. Like all fruits and vegetables, the tomato does contain a smidgen of fat but, of course, no cholesterol, and delivers a mere five calories per ounce, or about thirty calories in an average slicer.

Since the tomato provides vitamin A, it also contains one of its precursors, beta-carotene, which recently has become a buzzword because it is thought to lower the risk of cancer. It is now suspected that it is not only beta-carotene that offers cancer protection but also its cousins, the carotenoids. Among these relatives is one called lycopene, and the tomato—whether fresh or as tomato sauce, juice, or paste—contains more of it than any other produce (almost twice as much as second-ranking watermelon). The tomato, in fact, is the star of this particular show because it surpasses all other vegetables and fruits in total carotenoids, since over two-thirds of them come from lycopene. This is not to encourage you to think of the tomato (or any other food) as medicine, a mistake common in our culture, but to offer you yet another reason, should you need one, to freely indulge. When you consider how much taste is packed into a single good tomato, it's a real nutritional bargain.

Charley Rick told me the story of hearing of a man who claimed he lived exclusively on tomatoes. A wealthy man with food allergies, he traveled continuously, following tomato season. A nutritionist confirmed that the fellow's interestingly limited diet was possible, but added that he probably took a protein supplement. Most people can eat tomatoes with abandon, particularly if they do so without the addition of ingredients that alter the tomato's benign nutritional profile. Although allergies to the tomato itself are said to be rare, the pollen and the tiny hairs on the stems and foliage of the plant can cause a skin rash in some people. Additionally, there is substantial evidence that members of the nightshade family (potatoes, eggplants, tomatoes, peppers) aggravate the symptoms of rheumatoid arthritis, though without any apparent lasting effect or damage.

Nearly all kitchens in America have tomatoes in various forms in their cupboards and pantries. Whether it is a bowl brimming over with a rainbow of heirloom tomatoes or a cupboard stocked with ketchup and pasta sauce, we find tomatoes nearly everywhere that people cook, or simply eat. Even college students are likely to have a bottle of ketchup or a frozen pizza slathered with tomato sauce stashed away. The tomato serves us well, but with a bit of knowledge, this culinary workhorse will perform even more successfully.

When working with fresh tomatoes, the most important quality to understand is the effect of temperature. Their flavor begins to deteriorate when the thermometer drops below about 54 degrees Fahrenheit. So don't refrigerate your tomatoes. It is certainly tempting, especially as the harvest gets into full swing, to extend the life of all those extra tomatoes by chilling them. Unfortunately, it renders them tasteless and makes the flesh mealy as well. Try to use fresh tomatoes within three to four days, and if you can't, make a simple sauce or salsa that will hold in the refrigerator for a few extra days.

When it comes to the problematic half tomato, there is no satisfying answer. If it sits at room temperature, it will spoil rapidly. If you refrigerate it, it will lose its flavor. Why not just eat it? If you simply can't, chop it coarsely, cover it with either olive oil or vinegar, and use it the next day in a salad dressing or sauce.

When it comes to cooking with fresh tomatoes, the

guidelines are equally simple. To retain that bright, fresh flavor, cook tomatoes quickly. If they're cooked longer than about thirty minutes, their flavor begins to change as sugars are released and liquid evaporates. The resulting taste can be insipid. To transform this quality, tomatoes must undergo lengthy, slow cooking, a technique that applies to just a few recipes such as a traditional ragù, which contains beef. So the rule here is to cook tomatoes for a very short time or, on occasion—primarily when meat is an ingredient—for a very long time.

When should you peel tomatoes, and how? Any tomato with troublesome skin—too thick, scarred, or otherwise damaged—should be peeled, as should tomatoes for most sauces and for canning. For quick sauces and salsas, especially uncooked ones, it is up to you. Some people prefer their tomatoes peeled; others like that bit of resistance the skin offers. The same is true for tomatoes to be used in salads, though more people accept the skins here than in sauces. A peeled tomato is silkier and more elegant than an unpeeled one; let that quality be your guide. If a friend serves me a platter of sliced tomatoes from his garden, I expect that they will have their skins and that is fine with me. If I am served a fresh tomato salad in an expensive restaurant, I would prefer that the tomatoes be peeled.

To seed a fresh tomato, peeled or unpeeled, is simple. Cut it in half horizontally—that is, through its equator—hold each half over a bowl, cut side down, and gently squeeze out the seeds and gel, coaxing them out with your finger if necessary.

If you find you have particularly watery tomatoes on

hand, seed them, chop them coarsely, and then place them in a strainer and let them drain for ten to fifteen minutes. The addition of a bit of salt will speed up the release of water, but it is not absolutely necessary.

HOW TO PEEL A TOMATO Beware! Books and articles that tell you to plunge a tomato into a pot of boiling water for 30 to 60 seconds are wrong. Left in its bath for more than 15 seconds, your tomato will become mushy. Best is a 5- to 10-second dip; occasionally, a stubborn tomato will require 15 seconds, but only rarely. Even better is a quick scorching of the skins over a gas flame, the tomato stuck on the tines of a fork. Turn the fork quickly so that the flesh doesn't begin to cook; it takes about 5 to 15 seconds per tomato, depending on size. A water bath will dilute the flavor of the tomato slightly; the flame will intensify the taste. With either method, set the tomatoes aside until they are cool enough to handle; the skins will pull away easily, nearly by their own effort. Do not put tomatoes in a cold water bath to cool them; it will only further dilute the flavor. A well-grown, properly ripened tomato may not need the extra help; its skin should pull off easily with a sharp knife, though the process is a little slower than the water-dip or the direct-flame method. To encourage the skin to loosen, rub the tomato with the dull edge of a knife and then peel it. You may also peel certain varieties of tomatoes—firm-fleshed Romas, especially—using a standard vegetable peeler.

To purée fresh or canned tomatoes, use a food mill (see About Food Mills, page 64) rather than a food processor or blender. In one step, you will get a smooth, dense purée with the seeds and skins removed. If you purée in a blender or processor, you must then strain your sauce, which will be slightly foamy because of the way in which the blades of either machine incorporate air. *Never* purée fresh tomatoes in this way; the amount of foam created is unacceptable.

The guidelines for cooking with canned tomatoes are similar to the rules for working with the fresh fruit. It does not take long to make a simple, flavorful sauce or soup from good-quality canned tomatoes. To make a rich, meaty sauce with great depth of flavor, lengthy cooking over *extremely* low heat is necessary. Reliable recipes will recommend suitable cooking times, but be skeptical of those that call for an hour or so of simmering. That's too long for lighter sauces, yet doesn't allow enough time for the development of richer flavors.

Like fresh tomatoes, canned whole tomatoes should have their stem ends and seeds removed. This can be done quickly with a small, sharp knife or with your fingers; I prefer my fingers. Simply pull away the hard stem end and squeeze out the seeds and discard them. Passing the tomatoes through a food mill is an efficient way to separate the seeds, though the ends must be removed and the tomatoes broken up by hand first.

When using canned tomatoes, it is important to know your ingredients. Not all canned tomato products are of equal quality. Indeed, I find a great deal of variation, particularly among canned whole tomatoes. Many are mushy; some have a thin and insipid taste with slightly metallic undertones; others are overly acidic or too sweet. The amount of tomatoes per can varies a great deal, too; some have as few as seven or eight tomatoes; others have a dozen or more. The best way to discover the brand of canned tomatoes that works for you is to taste all that are available in your area and choose those that you like.

> *TO FIX A THIN SAUCE* *Although a sauce made primarily of tomato paste is too thick and unpleasantly cloying, tomato paste is ideal for rescuing a sauce or salsa that is too thin; it will add structure to such mixtures. To correct a thin sauce, stir in a teaspoon or two of double-concentrated tomato paste (available in convenient tubes), tasting after each addition, until you have achieved the proper consistency. This technique works with fresh, uncooked salsas as well as with cooked tomato sauces and soups. Just guard against adding too much paste or your sauce will take on its characteristics rather than retain the original recipe's flavors. I recommend no more than 2 teaspoons per cup of sauce.*

TASTING TOMATOES

The best way to learn about any food is to taste it. Whether you are trying to find a great olive oil, a good mustard, a perfect peach, or your favorite tomato, nothing substitutes for the immediate experience upon your palate. Of course, informed tasting is ideal, but knowledge cannot be substituted for direct experience. Certainly, it is important to have an intellectual understanding of the food in question, a knowledge of its ideal properties. Armed with these factual details, set out to find the fresh tomatoes and canned products that you like best.

In the culinary classes I teach at our local college, I give my students an assignment in comparative tomato tasting, and I am always astonished by the number of people for whom such an experience is a revelation. So many people have given up on the possibility of finding good-tasting tomatoes; they are resigned to the mealy commercial tomatoes sold year-round in supermarkets, forgetting that just off the main road are neighbors and farmers offering the real thing. Because the course is offered in the fall during the peak of the tomato harvest, a comparative tasting works perfectly. The students fill out their tasting forms for each of the tomatoes they've gathered—one from a major market, one from a legitimate farm stand or market, one from a home garden—and write an essay about the exercise. For the younger students, all too many of whom have been raised on a diet of fast food, the assignment is a revelation. It is often the first time they have tasted a "real" tomato. For older students, the exercise often brings back memories of tomatoes eaten as children, which is frequently the last time they tasted a tomato with backyard flavor. The exercise changes nearly all students' buying—and eating—habits.

Tasting a variety of tomatoes can offer a great deal of pleasure. Unlike certain organized tastings—olive oil, for example, or vinegar—a fresh-tomato tasting does not involve eating a food out of its normal context. Many people recoil at the idea of tasting a spoonful of oil or sucking on a sugar cube soaked in tart vinegar, but nearly everyone can appreciate the pleasure of a bite of tomato. The purpose of tasting tomatoes in this formal manner is to familiarize yourself with the particular characteristics of certain varieties. Because texture—and thus, shape—plays an essential role in how foods taste, I recommend tasting both slices and pieces of each tomato. Consider nuance of flavor, texture, and aroma, and be sure to pay attention to the tomato's color and the thickness of its skin. Commercially grown tomatoes often have thick, unpleasant skins; the skins of boutique tomatoes are generally thinner and more delicate, easy and pleasant to eat. After you taste a slice and a spoonful of diced tomatoes, add a little salt to a piece and see how that influences the flavor. A bit of salt on a fresh, raw tomato is essential, drawing out flavors on the tongue that might be missed without it. (If you have reservations about using salt, please read the sidebar on page 65.) At the conclusion of the tasting, toss the remaining tomatoes together as a salsa, salad, or fresh tomato sauce.

Consider tasting commercial canned tomatoes with a group of friends who share an interest in cooking. This way, several people can explore the various qualities and discover those brands they prefer. And afterwards, of course, the leftover tomatoes can be made into a sauce and you can end your tasting with a spaghetti lunch or dinner.

Taste in an organized fashion. After displaying the products to be tasted in the manner described in the tasting menus (pages 49–50), assess the tomatoes visually, one brand at a time, considering their color and consistency. Is the liquid surrounding the tomatoes thin and watery? Do the tomatoes appear to be mealy? Are the stem ends hard and green, or is the entire tomato a rich, ripe red? Are there blemishes or black spots? Note your reactions on the evaluation form before continuing.

Next, spoon a portion of the tomato product into your bowl, leaning close to catch the aroma. Does it smell fresh? Finally, taste the product, considering both texture and flavor. Is it silky, watery, mealy, oily? Does it taste like fresh tomatoes? Is there a bitter or metallic aftertaste? Is it too sweet or too acidic? Note all of these reactions on the evaluation form and then continue until you have evaluated all the brands of tomatoes. Discuss your reactions with the other tasters, and retain the information for reference.

MENUS FOR A TOMATO TASTING

To taste fresh tomatoes
For each taster provide:
  A small bowl of kosher (coarse-grain) salt
  A small glass plate and a fork
  A large glass of unflavored sparkling water
  An evaluation sheet (see Tasting Notes, page 288) and
    a pencil
  A napkin

On the common table place:
  One each (for cherry or currant tomatoes, a cluster) of
    up to twelve varieties of fresh tomatoes, either all of
    a similar type or all of a specific common quality
    (all cherry tomatoes, all orange tomatoes, all

tomatoes from a single garden, and so on), left
    whole
A glass plate displaying the same tomatoes sliced,
    placed in front of their corresponding whole
    tomatoes (cut cherry tomatoes and pear tomatoes in
    half)
A glass bowl displaying the same tomatoes cut into
    $1/2$-inch dice, placed in front of their corresponding
    whole tomatoes (this step is unnecessary for cherry
    tomatoes)
Bottles or pitchers of chilled sparkling water

To taste commercial canned tomato products

For each taster provide:
    Several small glass bowls
    1 or 2 plastic spoons
    Several unseasoned water crackers
    A large glass of unflavored sparkling water
    An evaluation sheet (see Tasting Notes, page 288) and
      a pencil
    A napkin

On the common table place:
    Up to 8 similar tomato products (all canned whole
      tomatoes, for example) in their containers
    Glass bowls filled with the product to be tasted, placed
      in front of their corresponding containers
    Large serving spoons for each product to be tasted
    Bottles or pitchers of chilled sparkling water
    A basket of unseasoned water crackers

PART TWO

The Annotated Tomato Pantry

A PROPERLY STOCKED PANTRY MAKES THE LIFE OF any cook simpler and more pleasant. How much more we can enjoy our kitchens when a good selection of basic ingredients is at hand! Certainly, exactly what those ingredients include will depend upon how much and what style of cooking you do, but there are certain items essential in every pantry: a selection of dried pastas; two or three types of rice; polenta; pure olive oil for cooking and extra-virgin olive oil for imparting flavor; a selection of vinegars; a good Dijon mustard; Tabasco sauce and red pepper flakes; kosher salt; and whole black peppercorns. With these and a few other items—notably, a diverse supply of tomato products—you can put together a basic yet delicious meal without a last-minute visit to the market.

How you stock your pantry with preserved tomato products will have a great deal to do not only with your daily cooking habits, but also with whether or not you have a garden. If you grow your own tomatoes, there is a good chance that your pantry shelves, and perhaps your freezer, too, will be filled with jars of home-canned tomatoes and tomato products. Lucky you. However, if you don't have a productive patch of land or the time to cultivate it, you will need to select an array of good tomato products to see you through the winter and spring.

It is easy to find good canned tomatoes, much easier than it is to buy a good fresh tomato. I recommend purchasing pure tomato products, those without the addition of

herbs, spices, and other flavorings so that you can add your own. It is important to get into the habit of reading labels, and you should look for tomato products that list only tomatoes, tomato juice, salt, and, occasionally, citric acid and basil. Other ingredients are unnecessary. These days market shelves offer a multitude of tomato products: tomatoes ground, crushed, quartered, sliced, diced, and stewed as well as left whole. Whole tomatoes with basil leaves have been quite common for years, but recently producers began appealing to Americans' increasingly adventurous palates, and tomatoes spiked with Mexican seasonings, Cajun spices, hot chipotle peppers, or other flavorings have been joining the more traditional offerings. A basil leaf tucked into a can of tomatoes is harmless enough, but in general I find that most of the other products have a somewhat artificial flavor that is difficult to mask. I ignore most of these canned tomatoes; I recommend that you do the same. Similarly, I suggest that you don't buy prepared pasta sauces and salsas, but instead make your own with quality canned products during the off-season.

THE WELL-STOCKED PANTRY

Any cook needs a good supply of tomato products in the pantry, not just for carefully planned menus and favorite recipes, but for those culinary emergencies that inevitably occur: unanticipated guests, a busy schedule, a sudden craving for spaghetti, an unexpected storm. With a shelf full of good canned tomatoes and just a few other ingredients, you can put together a quick meal without much effort. And often simply adding a small amount of tomato—a table-spoon or two of tomato paste, for example, or a squeeze of dried tomato purée in a tube—is just what a bland soup or sauce needs to perk it right up.

Finally, although home cooks have been creating all sorts of sauces in their kitchens for centuries and will continue to do so without ever opening a book, certain sauces follow long traditions, and their mere names can conjure up their subtle flavors. Here, the glossary includes a listing of these traditional sauces. You will find my variations of a few of them in Basic Sauces on pages 231–249.

THE WELL-STOCKED PANTRY

The reluctant cook will find these tomato products significantly ease the pain of putting together a meal at the last minute.

Ground (or crushed) tomatoes:
Perfect for a quick soup or spaghetti sauce

Tomato sauce:
Essential in many simple soups and sauces

Double-concentrated tomato paste in a tube:
Much less troublesome than a can of tomato paste—half of which invariably goes to waste—and so easy to use.

The culinary enthusiast will want to have these tomato products available at all times, not just as ingredients for familiar recipes but as a bit of inspiration when it's hard to decide what to cook. If you preserve your own tomatoes, substitute them for the products listed here.

Canned tomatoes:
Whole in juice; diced; chopped; ground or crushed; strained; sauce; double-concentrated paste

Dried tomatoes:
Marinated dried tomatoes; dried-tomato purée in a tube; dried-tomato bits

Other tomato products:
Juice; olive oil flavored with sun-dried tomatoes

A GLOSSARY OF COMMERCIAL TOMATO PRODUCTS AND TRADITIONAL TOMATO SAUCES

ALL'AMATRICIANA Traditional spicy Italian sauce for pasta, made with onions, pancetta, tomatoes, and hot peppers.

ANDALOUSE A *velouté* (classic white sauce made with chicken stock, veal stock, or fish fumet) seasoned with concentrated tomato purée, sweet peppers, and parsley.

ARRABBIATA Another charmingly named, traditional Italian tomato sauce, this one from the south. The name translates literally as "anger" or "rage," which refers to the substantial amount of red pepper flakes that characterize this pasta sauce.

AURORE A *velouté* seasoned with concentrated tomato purée.

BOLOGNESE See Ragù

CHORON A classic béarnaise sauce (a reduction of herbs, aromatics, wine, and vinegar emulsified with egg yolk and butter) flavored with concentrated tomato purée.

CONCASSÉ A condiment of fresh, uncooked tomatoes that have been peeled, seeded, and finely chopped. It is seasoned simply, generally only with salt, and can form the basis of other sauces.

COULIS The term once referred to sauces and gravies in general; today, a tomato coulis is a simple but intensely flavored reduction of fresh peeled and seeded tomato pulp that has been drained of its liquid and cooked briefly in butter or olive oil with garlic and herbs.

DOUBLE-CONCENTRATED TOMATO PASTE A reduction of tomato paste; thick and intensely-flavored. Italian versions available in tubes are convenient to use in small amounts and keep well in the refrigerator.

DRIED-TOMATO BITS Commercial dried tomatoes that have been ground into small pieces; excellent in vinaigrette, risotto, polenta, and in any recipe where uniform distribution of the dried tomatoes is important.

DRIED-TOMATO PURÉE Dried tomatoes that have been reconstituted and puréed and are frequently seasoned with herbs and olive oil; intensely flavored and convenient to use in a variety of recipes.

DRIED TOMATOES Tomatoes that have had their water extracted through exposure to dry heat; intensely flavored with a slightly leathery, chewy texture.

FONDUE A classic sauce of peeled, seeded, and chopped tomatoes, pressed through a sieve and cooked in butter until soft. It may contain various seasonings such as garlic, herbs, sweet pepper, and paprika.

KETCHUP The classic sweet condiment ubiquitous in the United States, where it is served automatically with hamburgers and french fries. Today, to be called ketchup a product must contain tomatoes, vinegar, and sugar; it must be labeled "artificial" if the sugar is omitted. Most ketchup also contains onions, salt, and spices (most commonly allspice, black pepper, cinnamon, cassia, cloves, cayenne pepper, ginger, mustard, and paprika). In Europe, the condiment was traditionally made with mushrooms or walnuts, but the sauce is thought to be of Chinese origin.

MARINARA The familiar quickly cooked tomato sauce seasoned with garlic and onions. Some sources say the name—literally, "of the sailors"—refers specifically to sailors coming into port in Naples with Italy's first tomatoes; others say it refers to the speed of preparation, suitable to sailors who were in a hurry to get back to work.

NANTUA A *velouté* made with fish fumet and flavored with either fresh tomatoes or tomato purée.

PORTUGAISE Sauce *espagnole* (classic brown sauce; one of the three "grand sauces" in classical cuisine) with ripe tomatoes, garlic, olive oil, and tomato sauce.

PUTTANESCA A spicy Italian sauce with capers, black olives, anchovies, oregano, garlic, and tomatoes. Translated literally, the name means "in the style of the whores."

RAGÙ Meat sauce from Bologna, frequently called Bolognese sauce; the richest of the classic tomato sauces. Marcella Hazan recommends three essential steps in making successful, authentic ragù: the meat must not be browned, merely cooked long enough to lose raw color; the meat must be cooked in milk before tomatoes are added; and the sauce must simmer as slowly as possible for a minimum of $3^1/_2$ hours; 5 is better, she says.

SALSA Although the word translates literally as "sauce," salsa is used nearly exclusively to designate variations of a spicy condiment of Mexico—traditionally, a mixture of tomatoes, onions, chilies, and cilantro. Today a "salsa" can be made with everything from chopped mangos to diced clams and roasted coconut, the word indicating that the mixture has some level of heat and is a condiment. In Italian cuisine, "salsa" simply means sauce (as in, say, *salsa alla Marinara*). With all of the cultural crossover today, there is occasional confusion.

STEWED TOMATOES Chunks of tomatoes seasoned with a variety of herbs and spices; commercially, one of the most popular canned tomato products in the United States.

SUN-DRIED TOMATOES Tomatoes that have been sliced and set in the hot sun long enough, generally two to three days, for their water to evaporate. Although these are virtually unavailable commercially, many products on the shelf, as well as recipe and menu items, read "sun-dried tomatoes." Chances are, they are not.

TOMATO PASTE Legally, the liquid obtained from mature red tomatoes or from the residue of tomatoes prepared for canning or juice. The liquid is concentrated, may be treated with both hydrochloric acid and sodium hydroxide, and can be seasoned with salt, spices, flavorings, or baking soda. The label must indicate these additions. Salt and basil are the two most common additions.

TOMATO PURÉE The liquid obtained from mature red tomatoes or from the residue of tomatoes prepared for canning or juice. The liquid is concentrated, but not to the degree that tomato paste is.

TOMATO SAUCE Tomato purée to which seasonings—especially, salt, pepper, dried garlic, and dried onions—have been added.

PART THREE

A Tomato Cookbook

COOKING WITH TOMATOES

What is a recipe, truly, if not an invitation? "Here is where I've gone," the cook who offers up a recipe says. "I liked it here and I think you will, too." From this perspective, a recipe is not simply a list of ingredients and a few instructions; it is a call to adventure, mapped by a fellow explorer who made the journey before you or who found a slightly different way of getting there. Certainly, following the recipes here to the letter will yield results worthy of the good ingredients you choose. But you also should use the recipes for inspiration, as I do when I curl up in bed at night with a cookbook rather than a novel. Let my ideas, my ways of enjoying the tomatoes that I love so thoroughly, trigger your own.

The recipes you find here are a mix of tradition and innovation. Some are my interpretations of classic recipes, beverages, sauces, soups, and condiments that have been with us for decades, adjusted to suit my palate, my cooking style, and the ingredients at hand. Others have been inspired by my environment, by the fact that I live in a virtual Garden of Eden when it comes to all things agricultural. There is an almost daunting supply of wonderful ingredients in California's Sonoma County, which provide a constant source of inspiration and renewal. From July through the end of October, tomatoes of every shape and color are in glorious abundance. The recipes featuring fresh tomatoes are a result of this bounty and the creativity it ignites.

The most important thing to keep in mind when working with these—or any other—recipes is to seek the best ingredients available. Treated with care and intelligence, a fine tomato is difficult to damage. Taking the time to find the highest quality foods will give you the best results.

I am frequently asked if my recipes are "low-fat," a designation with which I have no small degree of difficulty. Low-fat or no-fat foods are currently trendy, and prepared foods, recipes, and books that incorporate the designation into their name or title sell like, well, low-cal hot cakes. As with most trends, there is a good deal of misunderstanding of the concept; the designation is frequently no more than a marketing gimmick. And so, no, my recipes are not devised to be low-fat, a concept that implies to me that a cook is attempting to mimic the taste of a dish that is traditionally high in fat while reducing the actual amount. I do not use margarine, for example; there is ample evidence that it is at least as harmful as butter, if not more so. I do not make reduced-fat mayonnaise, nor do I substitute nonfat milk when cream is called for. My vinaigrettes include olive oil among the ingredients. I do believe that the foods we eat— good tomatoes, for example—need a lot less added fat than has been used in traditional cooking in this country, and my cooking style reflects this belief. Similarly, although I make no effort to create vegetarian meals just for the sake of it, a large number of my menus never include meat. I also make the assumption that my readers are informed, intelligent, and capable of maintaining a healthy diet, yet willing to indulge for the sheer pleasure of it now and then.

ABOUT FOOD MILLS *In the late '50s and early
'60s, electrical appliances became extremely fashionable.
Mechanical tools were replaced, and while I doubt many re-
gret that the electric mixer supplanted the hand-held rotary
beater, many useful items disappeared in favor of new inventions. For example, the potato ricer—which looks a little
like an oversized garlic press—is a simple yet useful tool
that gives a fluffy, uniform texture to cooked potatoes that
cannot be achieved by other means. Lately, it has made a
comeback, and ricers can now be found in many specialty
stores. Similarly, the food mill is experiencing a revival of
interest.*

*The food mill is a simple machine with a handle, a large
sievelike bowl fitted with a bladelike paddle attached to a
central hand crank. The paddle is connected by a screw frequently fitted with a wire spring on the underside that turns
close to the bowl, scraping off the purée as the paddle presses
it through the bowl's small holes. Most food mills are fitted
with hooks that allow the machine to rest on the bowl or pot
that will catch the purée. The machine comes apart for easy
cleaning and is simple to reassemble.*

*I believe a food mill is essential in making a good tomato
sauce. It strains out seeds and skins without grinding them
into the sauce, as a processor or blender will do. Most important, it purées without incorporating air. If you have
ever had a sauce that was unpleasantly foamy—and I find
them all the time, frequently in upscale restaurants—you
will understand what I mean here. A blender or food processor incorporates air as it grinds, purées, and emulsifies.
That is fine for certain foods—homemade mayonnaise, for
example, and vinaigrettes—but it is dreadful for most vege-*

table- and fruit-based sauces. In this book, nearly all the recipes that require straining or puréeing recommend that you use a food mill. They are inexpensive—the best are under fifty dollars— simple to clean, and easy to store. And if there's a power failure, you won't be left with a half-made sauce.

A NOTE ABOUT SALT All the recipes in this book were tested using kosher salt, a coarse-grain salt without additives. I use this salt because I prefer both its taste and its texture over regular fine-grain table salt. Because kosher salt is flakier and less dense than standard commercial salt, some adjustment in quantity may be necessary. A recipe that calls for one teaspoon of kosher salt may require only half or three quarters that amount of fine-grain salt.

Regarding salt in general, I do not recommend omitting it entirely unless you have a specific medical condition that is made worse with the intake of salt. Although the use of salt is currently out of favor, only an extremely small segment of the population is adversely affected by its consumption. Salt is an essential seasoning that heightens the taste of nearly all foods; savory foods do not reach their full flavor without its skillful application. Salt draws the disparate elements of a dish together and, because it melts slowly on the tongue, contributes to the harmonious blending of flavors and creates a pleasant finish on the palate.

Michele Anna Jordan,
The Good Cook's Book of Mustard

Dried-Tomato Mayonnaise   Stir 2 to 3 tablespoons puréed dried tomatoes into 1 cup homemade or best-quality commercial mayonnaise. This is excellent on chicken sandwiches and hamburgers, and adds a pleasant tang to creamy potato salads.

Dried-Tomato Canapes   Cut a baguette in thin slices and spread a bit of old-fashioned cream cheese or young chèvre on each slice. Top with a dried tomato that has been marinated in oil and drained. Garnish with a bit of Basil Mayonnaise (page 170), tapenade mayonnaise (page 143), or Aioli (page 254).

Chèvre with Garlic & Dried-Tomato Salsa   Place an 8-ounce log or pyramid of chabis or other young chèvre on a large serving platter, spoon warm Garlic & Dried-Tomato Salsa (page 270) over it, sprinkle with $1/2$ cup toasted walnuts, and serve immediately with hot bread, crackers, or tortilla chips.

Mozzarella with Garlic & Dried-Tomato Salsa   Arrange 2 or 3 dozen tiny fresh mozzarellas on a serving platter and spoon Garlic & Dried-Tomato Salsa (page 270) over them. Serve with toasted croutons.

Deviled Eggs with Dried Tomatoes   Peel 4 hard-boiled eggs and cut them in half. Scoop out the yolks, mash them with a fork, and mix in about 4 tablespoons Dried-Tomato

Mayonnaise (see first Little Recipe) and 1 tablespoon Dijon mustard. Spoon the mixture into the whites of the eggs and garnish with a few turns of black pepper and a thin strip of marinated dried tomatoes.

Stuffed Olives   Stuff pitted olives (any type you prefer, as long as the pits are removed) with strips of dried tomatoes marinated in olive oil. Cut the tomatoes into lengthwise strips about $3/8$ inch wide and 1 inch long and fit them into each olive, adding a caper to each if you like. Serve immediately. To hold these olives in a brine, see page 83.

Focaccia Squares   Make Basic Focaccia Dough (page 139) and when cooled cut it into $1^1/2$-inch squares. Top it with Tuna Mayonnaise (page 143) or tapenade mayonnaise (page 143), a halved cherry or small pear tomato, and a sprig of Italian parsley.

Cherry Tomatoes with Tuna Mayonnaise   Remove the stem end and scoop out the inside of about three dozen cherry tomatoes and fill them with Tuna Mayonnaise (page 143) mixed by hand. Top each stuffed tomato with a bit of grated hard-boiled egg.

Avocado & Tomato Salad   Cut 2 ripe avocados and two ripe tomatoes into $1/2$-inch pieces and toss them with some fresh chopped garlic (as much or as little as you want), a tablespoon or two of your favorite olive oil, and the juice of a lemon. Add some cilantro leaves, kosher salt, and several turns of black pepper, toss again, and serve.

Dried-Tomato & Chèvre Salad Toss together 2 cups of crumbled chèvre (chabis, for example), 12 halved dried tomatoes marinated in oil and cut in slivers, $1/4$ cup pitted Kalamata or Niçoise olives, $1/4$ cup extra-virgin olive oil, and the juice of $1/2$ lemon. Add several turns of black pepper, toss again, and serve on a bed of butter lettuce or mixed greens.

Broccoli with Dried-Tomato Butter Toss tender, steamed broccoli with a tablespoon or two of Dried-Tomato Butter (page 251), a little kosher salt, and several turns of black pepper and serve as a side dish with poultry. To serve as a main course, toss the broccoli with chunks of chicken sautéed in the butter and spread them over a mound of pasta (linguine is ideal) tossed with the pan juices from cooking the chicken.

Pasta with Wilted Greens & Warm Tomato-Olive Vinaigrette Place a large handful or two of fresh garden greens (I prefer a mixture of bitter greens like arugula and radicchio) in a large bowl. Top them with freshly cooked, hot pasta of any shape you prefer (drained quickly, not rinsed) and 3 or 4 tablespoons of the vinaigrette (page 252). Toss quickly and season with black pepper. This makes a perfect lunch or light dinner for one person.

Pasta with Dried-Tomato Pesto & Walnuts For two people, cook 6 ounces of dried pasta (linguine or spaghetti) until just done. Drain but do not rinse it and place it in a large bowl. Toss with about 5 to 6 tablespoons of Dried-Tomato

Pesto (page 246) and top with 3 to 4 tablespoons of chopped walnuts. Garnish with a sprig of fresh basil, if available. Serve immediately.

Chicken with Warm Tomato Vinaigrette Cut boned chicken into large chunks and sauté it quickly in a little olive oil over high heat. When the chicken is just done, toss it with one of the warm tomato vinaigrettes (pages 252–253) and serve immediately, accompanied by rice or pasta.

Grilled Chicken Marinate pieces of chicken (I prefer thighs) in Spicy Tomato Marinade (page 202) for 45 minutes. Remove each piece from the marinade, shake it off, and grill or broil the chicken. Serve topped with several spoonfuls of fresh marinade.

Chicken with Tomato Salsa & Pasta Cook a thin pasta such as spaghettini or linguine, allowing about 3 ounces dry pasta per person. Grill or broil boned chicken breasts and thighs and slice them. Drain the pasta, toss it with any of the salsas on pages 257–270, and top it with slices of chicken and more salsa. Serve immediately.

Ratatouille Pizza Next time you make ratatouille (page 172), reserve 2 to 3 cups for pizza topping. Make Pizza Dough (page 147), roll it out, and spread the ratatouille over the surface. Grill a spicy sausage, cut it in diagonal pieces, and place them on top of the pizza before baking. Bake for 15 to 20 minutes in a 425°F oven, remove from the oven, slice, and serve.

Pizza with Dried-Tomato Pesto, Chicken, & Broccoli
Make pizza dough (page 147) and roll it out. Thin about $1/4$ cup Dried-Tomato Pesto (page 246) with enough warm water or olive oil to make it easily spreadable and cover the surface of the pizza skin with it. Top it with chunks of quickly sautéed chicken, pieces of steamed broccoli, and a very light sprinkling of a cheese such as Fontina or Gruyère. Bake for 15 to 20 minutes in a 425°F oven, remove from the oven, slice, and serve.

Sautéed Tomatoes For 4 people, peel 4 medium tomatoes and cut them into wedges. Heat a little olive oil in a sauté pan and cook the tomatoes quickly, about 2 minutes on each side. Season them with a squeeze of lemon, salt, and black pepper. Scatter minced scallions over them, or top with some finely minced garlic and very thin strips of basil. Serve immediately as a side dish.

Grilled Scallions Rub a bunch of cleaned scallions (about 12) with a bit of olive oil and roast them in a 375°F oven or grill them on a stove top grill until they are limp and tender. Serve them wrapped in a warm corn tortilla or with white rice and plenty of Salsa Cruda (page 258), Garlic & Chive Salsa (page 259), or Winter Salsa (page 268).

Scalloped Potatoes Add $1/2$ cup diced dried tomatoes to your favorite scalloped potato recipe.

✿ Fresh Tomato Juice

Makes 6 to 8 cups

Commercial tomato juice is quite good, full of flavors and textures that are so familiar to us that sometimes a homemade version somehow tastes wrong. It is another thing entirely, and quite satisfying to make if you have a substantial supply of good tomatoes.

5 pounds very ripe toma-
toes, peeled, cored, and
seeded
1 small red onion, cut in
quarters
4 cloves garlic, peeled
2 ribs of celery, with leaves

1 small bay leaf
1 or 2 serrano peppers
4 sprigs of Italian parsley
1 teaspoon whole black
peppercorns
Kosher salt
Granulated sugar

Combine all of the ingredients except the salt and sugar in a heavy stockpot and set over medium heat. When the tomatoes come to a simmer, reduce the heat to low, cover the pot, and cook for 30 minutes. Remove from the heat and let cool for about 15 minutes. Discard the sprigs of parsley, the celery, and the peppers. Press the mixture through a food mill or sieve, discard the solids, and chill the juice. When the juice is thoroughly chilled, taste it and adjust the seasoning with a generous teaspoon of salt and a miserly $1/2$ teaspoon of sugar. Taste again, and add more salt or sugar as necessary for a balanced juice.

VARIATIONS:

1. Combine, cup for cup, tomato juice and sauerkraut juice. Season with toasted caraway seeds.

2. Combine, cup for cup, tomato juice and clam juice, and season with the juice of $1/2$ lemon, salt, and Tabasco sauce.

✿ Tomato Juice Cocktail

Serves 4

Here's a refreshing drink—mildly spicy and just slightly sweet—for a hot afternoon.

4 cups fresh tomato juice
   (preceding recipe)
1 cup fresh orange juice
Juice of 1 lime
2 tablespoons red wine
   vinegar, medium acid
2 cloves garlic, pressed

1 teaspoon celery salt
Several shakes of Worces-
   tershire sauce
Several drops of Tabasco
   sauce
Kosher salt and freshly
   ground black pepper

Mix together all the ingredients and taste the juice. Adjust the seasonings for salt, heat, and acid. Chill thoroughly and serve over ice.

🍅 Tomato-Cucumber Cocktail

Serves 4

*Cucumber adds a cool spark wherever it is used. For this refreshing drink,
you'll need a juice extractor.*

4 cups fresh tomato juice
  (page 71)
1 cup fresh cucumber juice
1/2 teaspoon celery salt
2 teaspoons finely minced
  lemon zest
1 tablespoon chives,
  snipped

Tabasco sauce
Kosher salt and freshly
  ground black pepper
8 long stalks of chive
4 thick strips of fresh
  cucumber, peeled and
  seeded
4 lemon slices

Mix together the tomato juice, cucumber juice, celery salt,
lemon zest, and snipped chives. Season to taste with Tabasco sauce, salt, and pepper. Pour into 4 glasses filled with
ice and garnish each serving with 2 long chives, a strip of
cucumber, and a lemon wedge.

 Bloody Mary

Few beverage traditions are as familiar to as many people as this classic.

Kosher salt

2¹/₄ teaspoons celery salt

Wedge of lemon

2 jiggers (3 ounces) best-quality vodka, chilled

Generous squeeze of fresh lemon juice

Several shakes of Worcestershire sauce

3 or 4 drops Tabasco sauce

1 teaspoon prepared horseradish

8 ounces homemade tomato juice (page 71), chilled

¹/₄ teaspoon fine-grain sea salt

¹/₈ teaspoon black pepper

Make the Bloody Mary in a large (16-ounce) glass. Mix the kosher salt with 2 teaspoons of the celery salt in a saucer or low bowl. Rub the rim of the glass with the wedge of lemon and dip it into the salt mixture so that it clings to the rim. Fill the glass with ice. Add the vodka and then the lemon juice, Worcestershire sauce, and Tabasco sauce. Stir in the tomato juice with a long spoon. Add the horseradish, sea salt, the remaining celery salt, and pepper. Stir again and serve.

VARIATIONS:

VIRGIN MARY: Omit the vodka.

BLONDIE: If you happen upon a cache of white tomatoes, make juice and then follow the recipe, omitting the Worcestershire sauce and using crushed white pepper instead of black pepper. Dazzling!

 Bloody Maria

With tequila and Mexican flavors, this spicy twist on the tradition is great with chips, salsa, and other casual fare.

¹/₂ lime, cut in 2 pieces
Kosher salt in a wide dish
2 jiggers (3 ounces) tequila
2 or 3 drops Habanero
  hot sauce, if available;
  other hot sauce, if not
¹/₂ teaspoon minced fresh
  cilantro

¹/₄ teaspoon celery salt
¹/₄ teaspoon fine-grain sea
  salt
8 ounces tomato juice,
  chilled
Sprig of cilantro, for
  garnish

Rub the rim of a large glass with a piece of lime and dip it into the kosher salt so that the salt sticks to the rim. Fill the glass with ice, add the tequila, followed by the hot sauce, cilantro, celery salt, and sea salt. Stir with a long spoon, add the tomato juice, and stir again. Add a squeeze of the remaining piece of lime, garnish with a sprig of cilantro, and serve immediately.

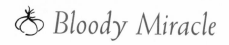 # Bloody Miracle

Serves 4 to 6

This lively cocktail comes to us from The Book of Garlic, *the charming treatise on the stinking rose by California author John Harris. Although you can certainly make a single serving, I recommend preparing a pitcher and enjoying it with friends during a leisurely summer brunch. After trying this version, you may never want another.*

1 lemon, cut in wedges
Kosher salt, for dipping
12 ounces best-quality
  vodka
6 cloves garlic, pressed
1 tablespoon Tabasco
  sauce

1/2 cup fresh lemon juice
2 teaspoons celery salt
1 teaspoon black pepper
1 teaspoon kosher salt
32 ounces (1 quart)
  tomato juice
Sprigs of cilantro

Rub the rims of the glasses with the lemon wedges and then dip them in the kosher salt. Fill a large pitcher half full of ice. Add the vodka, garlic, Tabasco sauce, lemon juice, celery salt, pepper, and kosher salt. Stir the mixture with a long spoon, add the tomato juice, and stir again. Garnish each glass with a sprig of cilantro and fill. Serve immediately.

APPETIZERS

🧅 Tomato Granita with Serrano Peppers & Cilantro

Serves 8

Serve this luscious tomato ice as an appetizer or between courses to freshen the palate.

3 pounds ripe red or
   golden tomatoes
1 or 2 serrano peppers
4 tablespoons finely
   minced fresh cilantro

Juice of 1 lime
Pinch of kosher salt
Pinch of sugar
Cilantro sprigs for garnish

Peel the tomatoes and remove the cores. Cut the tomatoes in half and squeeze out the seeds and excess juice. Grind the tomatoes through a food mill into a large bowl. Remove the stems and seeds of the serrano peppers and mince the peppers very finely. Add them to the tomatoes along with the cilantro and lime juice. Stir and taste the mixture. Add a bit of salt or a bit of sugar to adjust the flavor, if necessary: if the tomatoes are bland, add the salt; if they are too acidic, add a bit of sugar. Pour the liquid into two metal ice-cube trays or into a 9- by 13-inch baking dish and place in the freezer for at least 5 hours, until the mixture is frozen solid. (Or freeze it in a commercial ice-cream maker according to the manufacturer's instructions.) An hour before serving, re-move it from the freezer, break it into chunks, place it in a food processor, and pulse quickly until the mixture is slushy. Place it in individual serving dishes and return it to the freezer for up to 1 hour before serving. Garnish each dish with a small sprig of fresh cilantro.

🍅 Bloody Mary Sorbet

Serves 6 to 8

The time to serve this sassy sorbet is when the temperature climbs into the high 90s and low 100s and there's not a hint of a breeze.

4 cups fresh tomato juice
    (page 71) or commercial
    tomato juice
Juice of 2 lemons
Several shakes of Worces-
    tershire sauce
1 tablespoon prepared
    horseradish
$1/2$ teaspoon ground cumin

$3 1/4$ teaspoons Tabasco
    sauce or more to taste
$1/2$ teaspoon celery salt
1 teaspoon fine-grain sea
    salt
1 teaspoon black pepper
Best-quality vodka, chilled
    in the freezer
Sprigs of celery or fresh
    herbs, for garnish

Mix together the tomato juice, lemon juice, Worcestershire sauce, horseradish, cumin, Tabasco sauce, celery salt, sea salt, and pepper and stir the mixture well. Taste it and adjust the seasonings. Chill it thoroughly and then freeze it in a commercial ice-cream maker according to the manufacturer's instructions. Alternately, chill it in a low, metal baking dish in the freezer until solid, at least 4 hours. Remove the mixture from the freezer, break it into pieces, place it in a food processor. Pulse briefly, until the juice is slushy. Transfer the sorbet to individual serving dishes and return it to the freezer until firm, or up to 1 hour. Remove it from the freezer and top each serving with a jigger of chilled vodka and a sprig of celery or herbs.

🌼 Tomato Bruschetta with Six Variations

Serves 6 to 8

Italian by tradition, this simple appetizer has become immensely popular in the United States, where it appears on menus, in cookbooks, at backyard barbecues, all for good reason: it is delicious, and one of the best and simplest uses of summer tomatoes.

1 loaf country-style bread such as sourdough, or Italian, cut into thick slices

3 medium ripe red tomatoes

Kosher salt and freshly ground black pepper

Several cloves of garlic, cut in half

Best-quality extra-virgin olive oil

Grill or toast the bread. While it is cooking, peel and seed the tomatoes, chop them coarsely, and season them with a little salt and pepper. Rub one side of each slice of bread with a piece of garlic and place the bread on a large platter. Drizzle each slice with a generous tablespoon of olive oil and top with a large spoonful of the chopped tomatoes Serve immediately.

VARIATIONS:

ANCHOVY: Drape each slice of finished bruschetta with an anchovy fillet.

MOZZARELLA: While toasting or grilling the bread, top each piece (after turning once) with a thin slice of fresh mozzarella.

CHERRY TOMATOES & CHIVES: Instead of using large tomatoes, cut cherry tomatoes or small pear tomatoes in half and scatter them over the bruschetta. Top with snipped fresh chives.

RED ONIONS: Add 1 small red onion, minced, to the tomatoes. Top with finely chopped Italian parsley.

BASIL: Slice several leaves of basil into very thin strips and sprinkle them on the bruschetta just before serving.

BALSAMIC VINEGAR: Add 1 tablespoon balsamic vinegar to the tomatoes and top the bruschetta with a mix of fresh herbs (Italian parsley, oregano, thyme).

🍅 Filled Cherry Tomatoes with Seven Variations

Makes 24 pieces

Stuffed cherry tomatoes make great appetizers, single bites that can be filled with any number of great things. Of course, they can be dreadful if poor-quality tomatoes are used, so be sure to know your tomatoes before you plan your menu.

TECHNIQUES:

BASIC TECHNIQUE: Cut the stem end of each cherry tomato about $1/8$ inch down, just before you get to the wide shoulder of the tomato. Discard the end and use your finger, a grapefruit knife, or a tiny spoon to flick out the seeds. Set the tomatoes cut side down on absorbent toweling until ready to fill them.

TECHNIQUE VARIATION: When filling pear-shaped cherry (or larger) tomatoes, cut them in half lengthwise and use a small spoon to scoop out the seeds. Let the tomatoes rest cut side down on absorbent toweling until ready to fill them.

TO FILL: For smooth fillings like Tuna Mayonnaise (page 143) or cheese mixtures, place the filling in a pastry bag with a medium star tip and pipe the filling into each tomato. For chunky fillings like salsa, simply fill with a small spoon.

FILLINGS:

DRIED-TOMATO CREAM CHEESE: Mix together 4 tablespoons puréed sun-dried tomatoes with about 6 ounces (approximately 1 cup) cream cheese or young goat cheese. Season with a little fresh or dried thyme, black pepper, and kosher salt.

PESTO CREAM CHEESE: Mix together $1/4$ cup pesto with 6 ounces cream cheese or young goat cheese. Pipe the cheese mixture into the tomatoes and garnish each with a small fresh basil leaf.

CHÈVRE WITH FRESH HERBS & BLACK PEPPER: Mix 5 to 8 ounces of young chèvre such as chabis with 3 tablespoons minced fresh herbs and a tablespoon of freshly crushed black pepper. Pipe the mixture into tomatoes.

CORN SALSA: Use Grilled Corn Salsa (page 266) as a filling.

AVOCADO, RADISHES, & LIME JUICE: In a food processor, purée 1 ripe avocado with the juice of 1 lime (about 3 tablespoons juice). Transfer the avocado to a mixing bowl and fold in $1/2$ cup chopped radishes, 2 teaspoons minced cilantro leaves, 1 teaspoon minced jalapeño pepper, and salt and black pepper to taste. Spoon the mixture into cherry tomatoes.

SUMMER SQUASH SALSA WITH CHIPOTLE MAYONNAISE: Make the Summer Squash Salsa on page 267 and spoon it into halved plum tomatoes. Top with a bit of Chipotle Mayonnaise (page 255).

🧅 Marinated Olives Stuffed with Dried Tomatoes

Makes 1 quart

Dried tomatoes and olives make happy companions, to no small degree because of the Mediterranean heritage of both. We find them together in sauces and tapenades, on sandwiches, tucked into fish fillets and legs of lamb. Here, one is tucked into the other and they are then left to marinate in a spicy brine so that their flavors can meld. Serve these olives with good, hot bread, a creamy cheese, and a fruity red wine.

12 ounces (2 6-ounce cans) large black, green, or green-ripe olives, pitted

1 8-ounce jar dried tomatoes marinated in olive oil

1 jar capers

15 cloves garlic, peeled

2 teaspoons black peppercorns

1 teaspoon white mustard seed

2 bay leaves

1 small sprig fresh thyme

1 small sprig fresh oregano

3 long strips of orange zest

2 long strips of lemon zest

$1/4$ cup white wine or champagne vinegar

2 tablespoons salt dissolved in 2 cups spring water

Drain the olives of their brine and set them on a tea towel or absorbent paper. Drain the marinated tomatoes, reserving the oil. Cut the tomatoes in wedges that will fit easily into the olives. The actual size will vary depending on the olive, so experiment to see what works best. Drain the capers and place a single one into each olive, followed by a strip of dried tomato. Place the stuffed olives into a scalded glass quart jar or a clean crockery bowl. Repeat until all olives have been stuffed, adding a few cloves of garlic to the jar intermittently with the olives. If there are any leftover strips of tomatoes, add those to the jar. Add the peppercorns and mustard seed, and then tuck the bay leaves, sprigs of herbs, and zests down into the jar. Combine the vinegar and the salted water and pour the mixture over the olives. Float the reserved oil on top of the liquid so that it covers the surface. Cover the jar or bowl and refrigerate the olives for 1 week before using. Drain them before serving, and use them within 3 weeks.

🧅 Prawns with Tomato Essence, Olive Oil, & Basil

I love the delicate flavor of the tomato essence in this dish, which is perfect as a light main course during hot weather.

1/2 cup fresh basil leaves
  (loosely packed)
2/3 cup Tomato Essence
  (page 235), chilled
1/2 cup good-quality extra-
  virgin olive oil

Kosher salt and freshly
  ground black pepper
1 pound prawns, cooked,
  peeled, and deveined

Cut half of the basil leaves into very thin strips. Mix together the olive oil, tomato essence, and strips of basil, and add salt and pepper to taste. Toss the prawns with half of the sauce and arrange them on a serving platter. Pour the rest of the sauce over the prawns and garnish with the remaining basil leaves and a sprinkle of black pepper.

🧅 Dolmas with Tomato-Lemon Sauce

Makes about 6 dozen dolmas

Although these dolmas are not, strictly speaking, traditional, they evoke the flavors and aromas of classical Middle Eastern cuisine. I have been making them for over twenty years, and they remain one of my favorite appetizers. The tart and tangy tomato-lemon sauce is the element that ties all the other flavors together.

1 pound ground lamb
5 cloves garlic, minced
1 medium eggplant, peeled and cut into ¹/₂-inch cubes
³/₄ cup pine nuts, toasted
3 tablespoons Kalamata olives, pitted and minced
2 tablespoons preserved lemons, minced, plus ¹/₄ cup in wedges, as optional garnish (see Note)

2 tablespoons chopped fresh mint leaves
2 teaspoons chopped fresh oregano
Kosher salt and freshly ground black pepper
2 8-ounce jars of grape leaves in brine, drained and rinsed
Tomato-Lemon Sauce (page 245)

In a heavy skillet, sauté the lamb, breaking it up with a fork, until it is just loses its color but does not brown. Add the garlic and sauté for an additional 2 minutes. Add the cubes of eggplant and sauté over low heat until the eggplant is very soft and tender. Remove from the heat and stir in the pine nuts, olives, preserved lemons, half the mint, and the oregano. Taste the mixture and season it with a little salt and pepper. The filling and the sauce may be made a day in advance and refrigerated. Remove them from the refrigerator about 30 minutes before using.

To fill the dolmas, place a leaf, dull side up, on your work surface. Put about 2 teaspoons of filling in the center of the leaf. Fold the bottom of the leaf up over the filling and fold the two sides, one after the other, toward the center and over the top of the filling. Roll the bundle up to the tip of the leaf and place it seam side down in a shallow baking pan. Repeat until all the grape leaves have been filled.

Place the dolmas in a shallow baking pan. Ladle the sauce over them and bake them in a 325°F oven for about 20 minutes. Remove them from the oven and garnish them with the remaining chopped mint and, if using, the wedges of preserved lemons. Serve immediately.

Note: To make preserved lemons, wash and thoroughly dry 3 or 4 organic lemons, preferably Meyer variety, and cut each one into 8 wedges. In a nonreactive bowl, mix together $1/4$ cup kosher salt and 2 teaspoons sugar. Toss the lemon wedges in the mixture and then transfer them to a clean pint jar. Pour $1/3$ cup fresh lemon juice over them, cover the jar tightly, and keep it in a cool, dark cupboard for 5 to 7 days, turning it upside down each morning and righting it at night, so that all of the lemons spend time in the liquid. Use the lemon slices immediately, or top off the jar with mustard oil or extra-virgin olive oil. Store the jar in the pantry for up to 4 weeks, in the refrigerator for up to 2 months.

 Striped Tomato Brie

Serves 6 to 8

This simple appetizer, originally developed by Ruth Waltenspiel of Timber Crest Farms, can be made several days in advance and kept in the refrigerator. It is especially convenient in the summer or around the holidays when unexpected guests may stop by. Be sure the Brie you use is not too ripe; a fully ripened cheese will not hold together for filling and reassembly.

2 round, semi-ripe 8-ounce Brie cheeses, chilled

1/2 cup Dried-Tomato Butter (page 251), room temperature
1 cup toasted walnuts, finely chopped

To cut the chilled Brie in half, you will need a piece of dental floss (waxed is best) about 2 feet long. Set one of the cheeses on your work surface. Wrap the floss around it horizontally, positioning it in the middle of the narrow edge of the cheese. Gather both ends of the floss in your right hand, holding close to the cheese. Use your left hand to keep the cheese steady, and with your right hand gently pull the dental floss through the cheese, cutting it in half. (Reverse hands if you are left-handed.) Separate the halves, placing them with the inside up on your work surface. Cut the second Brie.

On the surface of one side of each of the cheeses, spread about 1/8 inch of the Dried-Tomato Butter. Top with the second half of each cheese. Spread the outer circumference of each with a thin coating of the butter and then dip the buttered edge in the chopped walnuts so that they stick and form a crustlike coating around the outer edge of the cheese. Serve the cheese immediately with crackers or slices of baguette, or wrap it tightly and store in the refrigerator for up to 5 days or in the freezer for up to 3 weeks. Remove it from the refrigerator 30 minutes before serving, from the freezer at least 2 hours beforehand.

SOUPS

GAZPACHO

Today, the Spanish-style soup we call *gazpacho* most nearly resembles a sort of chunky liquid salad, with lots of fresh, uncooked vegetables suspended in a broth of puréed tomatoes or tomato juice and chicken stock. In summer when all of the vegetables are at their finest, this simple, modern soup is full of refreshing good flavor. It is a distant cousin, however, of this peasant fare as it first developed. Farther still from the original are the more complex contemporary versions that include everything from clam juice, lobster, and shrimp to raisins, walnuts, mangos, and melons. Many chefs adopt the word to describe any uncooked, chilled soup. It began as another thing entirely, and to forget its genesis is to lose the subtle elements that make today's gazpacho an evocatively refreshing summer meal.

The basic peasant staples of bread, garlic, olive oil, and vinegar evolved in several ways that remain with us today. In Italy, we find both bread salad and bread soup, historical cousins to the Andalusian soup featuring the same ingredients, the many variations of which came to be called *gazpacho*. Although the exact origin of the word is unknown, most sources suggest that it refers to fragments, crumbs, remnants of food—primarily, stale bread and bread crumbs—that were combined with vinegar, water, oil, garlic, and other seasonings and served at room temperature. Today, *gazpacho* remains true to its spiritual, if not culinary, roots in that it is one of the finest uses for too many ripe vegetables that might otherwise go to waste. And the original ingredients, especially vinegar, olive oil, and garlic, remain essential to a successful *gazpacho*. (For a more detailed story of the evolution of gazpacho, see *Why We Eat What We Eat* by Raymond Sokolov.)

 Red Gazpacho

Serves 4 to 6

This full-bodied version of contemporary gazpacho is best at the peak of harvest, when all of the vegetables are dazzlingly ripe. And on a hot day, there is nothing more refreshing.

4 or 5 large ripe tomatoes, peeled, seeded, and chopped
1 serrano pepper, minced
5 cloves garlic, minced
2 lemon cucumbers, peeled, seeded, and diced
1 red bell pepper, seeded and diced
1 red onion, peeled and thinly sliced
1 ripe but slightly firm avocado, peeled and diced
4 cups light beef stock or chicken stock
2 tablespoons fresh lemon juice
2 tablespoons medium-acid red wine vinegar
2 tablespoons chopped fresh basil
2 tablespoons chopped fresh Italian parsley
4 tablespoons chopped fresh cilantro
Kosher salt and freshly ground black pepper
1/2 cup best-quality extra-virgin olive oil

Combine all of the vegetables in a large bowl. Add the stock, lemon juice, and vinegar and stir very briefly. Stir in the fresh herbs and season with salt and pepper to taste. Chill the soup for at least 1 hour before serving. Remove the gazpacho from the refrigerator, stir, let it rest for 15 minutes, and then pour the olive oil over it and serve.

Golden Gazpacho

Serves 4 to 6

Certain varieties of golden tomatoes have a rich, velvety texture. This soup highlights that luscious quality.

4 or 5 ripe golden or
   orange tomatoes
3 cups homemade chicken
   stock
1 small red onion, minced
2 teaspoons finely minced
   garlic
Juice of 1 lime

Kosher salt and freshly
   ground black pepper
1 ripe avocado, peeled
   and sliced
4 to 6 tablespoons best-
   quality extra-virgin
   olive oil
2 tablespoons fresh
   minced chives

Peel the tomatoes and gently remove their seeds. Chop the tomato flesh very finely or pass it through a food mill (do not purée in a blender or processor) and place it in a large bowl. Stir in the stock, onion, garlic, and lime juice. Taste the soup and season with salt and pepper. Fold in the avocado and chill the soup for at least 1 hour. Remove the gazpacho from the refrigerator, ladle it into soup bowls, and top each serving with a generous tablespoon of olive oil and a sprinkling of chives.

❦ Smoky Gazpacho

Serves 4

This version brings a subtle smoky note to the crisp flavors and textures of gazpacho, an effect enhanced by the sherry vinegar.

1 medium red onion or 3 small red torpedo onions	3 tablespoons sherry vinegar
2 sweet red peppers	2 tablespoons chopped fresh herbs (marjoram, oregano, Italian parsley, chives, thyme)
6 large ripe tomatoes, smoked (page 236)	
6 cloves garlic, minced	
2 small cucumbers, peeled, seeded, and diced	$1/2$ cup extra-virgin olive oil
2 small zucchini, diced	1 cup fresh bread crumbs, toasted
1 cup chicken stock	

Remove the root end and papery skin of the onions. Roast the onions and peppers on a grill or under a broiler, turning often, until the skins of the peppers are charred and the onions are browned and partially cooked. Place the peppers in a paper bag until cooled, about 20 minutes. While the peppers are cooling, prepare the remaining vegetables. Peel, seed, and chop the tomatoes coarsely. Place all but $3/4$ cup of the chopped tomatoes in a large, nonreactive bowl. Chop the grilled onions and add them to the bowl with the tomatoes, along with the garlic, cucumbers, and zucchini.

Remove the charred skins, stems, and seeds from the peppers. Cut one pepper into chunks and place it in a blender, along with the reserved tomatoes and the chicken stock. Process until the mixture is smooth. Strain it through a sieve into the vegetables. Cut the remaining pepper into small dice and add it to the soup, along with the vinegar and fresh herbs. Chill the gazpacho for at least 2 hours before serving. Ladle it into soup bowls and top each serving with a healthy splash of olive oil and a scattering of bread crumbs.

🧅 Yogurt & Tomato Soup

Serves 6 to 8

This refreshing, soothing soup is both rich-tasting and low in fat and is very nearly a gazpacho, except for the yogurt that replaces the traditional broth.

2 cups plain yogurt
6 cups fresh tomato juice
3 tablespoons extra-virgin
   olive oil
4 tablespoons lemon juice
4 tablespoons red wine
   vinegar, medium acid
3 cucumbers, peeled,
   seeded, and chopped
1 or 2 jalapeño or serrano
   peppers, stems removed,
   finely minced

Kosher salt and freshly
   ground black pepper
2 tablespoons minced
   Italian parsley
2 tablespoons minced
   cilantro
2 tablespoons minced mint
2 teaspoons fine lemon
   zest

Mix together the yogurt, tomato juice, olive oil, lemon juice, and vinegar. Stir in the cucumbers and peppers, taste the soup, and season with salt and pepper. Combine the parsley, cilantro, mint, and lemon zest and stir the mixture into the soup. Chill the soup at least 2 hours before serving.

# Tomato Broth with Tiny Pasta

Light and fragrant, this delicate broth with its seedlike pasta is pure pristine pleasure.

2 tablespoons pure olive
   oil
1 yellow onion, peeled
   and diced
5 cloves garlic, minced
3 cups tomatoes, peeled,
   seeded, chopped
1 cup Tomato Essence
   (page 235)

3 cups stock (chicken,
   smoked chicken, or
   smoked duck)
6 ounces tiny seed pasta
1/4 cup Pernod
Kosher salt and freshly
   ground pepper
1/4 cup thinly sliced fresh
   basil leaves

Heat the olive oil in a heavy skillet and sauté the onion until it is tender and fragrant, about 15 minutes. Add the garlic and sauté another 2 minutes. Stir in the tomatoes, tomato essence, and stock and simmer over low heat for 10 minutes. Add the seed pasta and simmer until done, about 4 more minutes. Add the Pernod, taste the soup, and season with salt and pepper as needed. Ladle into warmed soup bowls. Top each serving with some of the fresh basil leaves. Serve immediately.

 Tomato-Cilantro Soup

Serves 6

I love this soup, and once served gallons of it in a small restaurant I operated in Sonoma County. It couldn't be simpler to make, yet its bright, refreshing taste keeps everyone coming back for more. In the off-season, make it with canned tomatoes.

1 medium yellow onion, chopped
$^1/_4$ cup pure olive oil
5 cloves garlic, minced
2 cups chicken stock
3 to 4 pounds red ripe tomatoes, peeled, seeded, and chopped

1 tablespoon Madeira (optional)
1 large or 2 small bunches fresh cilantro
Kosher salt and freshly ground black pepper
Cilantro sauce (see Note)

Sauté the onion in the olive oil until it is very soft, about 20 to 25 minutes, and add the minced garlic just before the last 2 minutes. Stir in the chicken broth. Add the tomatoes and stir well. Simmer for about 15 minutes. Remove the soup from the heat. Purée it with an immersion blender or in a container blender. Add the Madeira and cook over low heat for 5 minutes. Remove the cilantro leaves from the large stems and chop the leaves finely. Stir the cilantro into the soup, taste, and season with salt and pepper. Serve immediately, garnished with a spoonful of cilantro sauce.

Note: To make cilantro sauce, place 6 cloves of peeled garlic, 1 stemmed jalapeño or serrano pepper, and 1 bunch of cilantro, stems discarded, in a blender or food processor. Add $^1/_4$ cup fresh lime juice, 3 tablespoons extra-virgin olive oil, and 1 teaspoon kosher salt. Process until smooth. This sauce will keep in the refrigerator for 3 to 4 days.

🧅 Yogurt Soup with Tomato Oil

Serves 4 to 6

I find this soup evocative and refreshing, particularly on hot summer mornings when I serve it chilled.

3 tablespoons pure olive oil

3 yellow onions, peeled and diced

$1/2$ cup Tomato Essence (page 235)

$1/2$ cup extra-virgin olive oil

Kosher salt and freshly ground black pepper

3 cups homemade chicken stock

3 cups plain yogurt

1 cup Tomato Concassé (page 231)

$1/2$ cup cilantro leaves, chopped

$1/4$ cup mint leaves, chopped

Heat the olive oil in a heavy pot and sauté the onions over low heat until they are tender and fragrant and beginning to caramelize, about 25 to 30 minutes.

Meanwhile, make the tomato oil by mixing together the tomato essence and olive oil and season to taste with salt and pepper.

Add the chicken stock to the caramelized onions, bring it to a simmer, and stir in the yogurt until it is just heated through. Then stir in the concassé, cilantro, and mint. Remove from the heat, taste the soup, and add salt and pepper as needed. Either serve the soup immediately or first chill it thoroughly. Drizzle 2 tablespoons of the tomato oil on each serving.

🧅 Hearty Summer Tomato Soup

Serves 6 to 8

When you want a more substantial soup that still features the bright taste of summer tomatoes, this is the one.

^{1}/$_3$ cup light olive oil
2 yellow onions, sliced
3 large shallots, chopped
2 cloves garlic, chopped
2 carrots, peeled and sliced
2 ribs celery, heavy strings removed, sliced
Parsley sprigs
1 teaspoon sugar
Juice of 1 lemon
1 cup dry white wine

5 cups chicken or duck stock
4 pounds very ripe red tomatoes, peeled, seeded, and coarsely chopped
3 tablespoons tomato paste
Kosher salt and freshly ground black pepper
^{1}/$_2$ cup fresh herbs, finely minced (chives, cilantro, Italian parsley, oregano, basil, thyme, marjoram)

Heat the olive oil in a large, heavy pot, add the onions and shallots, and cook over medium heat until the vegetables are soft and fragrant, about 15 minutes. Add the garlic and cook 2 minutes. Add the carrots, celery, parsley sprigs, sugar, and lemon juice. Stir to blend the mixture, lower the heat, cover, and cook until all the vegetables are tender, about 15 minutes. Pour in the white wine and simmer over medium heat until the wine has nearly evaporated. Add 2 cups of the broth, remove from heat, and discard the parsley. Purée the mixture with an immersion blender.

Add the chopped tomatoes to the puréed vegetable mixture, stir in the tomato paste, and simmer over low heat for 15 minutes, stirring occasionally so the soup does not burn. Stir in the remaining stock, simmer 30 minutes, and taste the soup. Add salt and pepper as needed. Ladle the soup into warmed bowls and top each serving with a sprinkling of fresh herbs.

🧅 Tomato & Bread Soup

Serves 4

I love this traditional Italian soup and prepare it frequently in the winter, when I enjoy it by a hot fire. It takes barely any time at all to prepare and is an outstanding example of the influence of casual Italian fare on the way that we eat.

Extra-virgin olive oil
Handful of garlic cloves, peeled and chopped
4 cups ripe red tomatoes (about 2 pounds), peeled, seeded, and coarsely chopped, or an equivalent amount of canned diced or crushed tomatoes

4 cups homemade chicken stock
Black pepper in a mill and kosher salt
About 3 cups good, crusty day-old bread, torn or cut into 1-inch pieces
4 tablespoons chopped Italian parsley
Parmigiano cheese (optional)

Sauté the garlic in olive oil. Add the fresh tomatoes and simmer 3 to 5 minutes. Add the chicken stock, along with several turns of black pepper, and salt to taste. Divide the bread between the soup bowls and ladle the soup over the bread. Let the soup sit for about 5 minutes so that it cools a little and the bread soaks up some of the juices. Just before serving, drizzle each portion with a tablespoon or two of olive oil, a tablespoon of parsley, and a few turns of black pepper. If using, the cheese, top each serving with a generous grating of it.

✿ *Summer White Bean &* *Tomato Soup*

Serves 4 to 6

Although most bean soups are best in winter when their hearty creaminess warms and comforts us, this version is light enough to be wonderful in the summer months.

8 ounces dry white beans (Great Northerns or small whites)
¹/₄ pound pancetta
2 tablespoons pure olive oil
2 large shallots, minced
4 cloves garlic, crushed and minced

3 cups Tomato Essence (page 235)
3 cups homemade chicken or duck stock
Kosher salt and freshly milled pepper
¹/₄ cup minced fresh herbs (thyme, marjoram, oregano, summery savory, Italian parsley)

Soak the beans overnight in enough water to cover them, plus 2 inches. Rinse and drain the beans, place them in a heavy pot, cover them with fresh water, and simmer them over medium heat for about 25 minutes, until they are nearly tender. Drain and rinse the beans.

In a heavy skillet, sauté the pancetta in 1 tablespoon of the olive oil until it is almost crisp. Remove the pancetta from the pan and set it on absorbent paper. Add the remaining tablespoon of oil to the pan and sauté the shallots until they are tender and fragrant. Add the garlic and sauté another 2 minutes. In a large pot, heat the tomato essence and stock. Stir in the beans and the shallot-and-garlic mixture and simmer together for 15 minutes, covered. Chop the pancetta and add it to the soup. Season with the salt and several turns of black pepper to taste. Ladle the soup into warmed bowls and sprinkle the fresh herbs over each serving.

🧅 Tomato & Corn Chowder with Salmon, Fresh Ginger, & Lemongrass

Serves 6

The flavors of lemongrass and fresh ginger offer an intriguing element to this dazzling summer soup, perfect on a special occasion.

4 tablespoons pure olive oil
1 yellow onion, peeled and diced
3 cloves garlic, minced
1 serrano pepper, stem removed, finely minced
2-inch piece of ginger, peeled, chopped, and squeezed through a garlic press
1 quart fish stock, hot (see Note)
2 stalks lemongrass, bruised and cut into 1-inch pieces

Juice of 1 lime
$1/2$ cup white wine (sauvignon blanc)
2 medium tomatoes, peeled, seeded, and diced
1 cup fresh corn kernels
1 pound salmon fillet, skinned and cut in 1-inch cubes
$3/4$ cup heavy cream
$1/4$ cup cilantro leaves
Kosher salt and freshly milled black pepper

Heat the olive oil in a heavy pot and sauté the onions over medium heat until they are transparent and fragrant, about 15 minutes. Add the garlic and sauté another 2 minutes. Stir in the minced pepper and the ginger and pour the mixture into the hot soup stock. Add the lemongrass, lower the heat, cover the pot, and simmer 15 minutes. Add the lime juice, wine, and tomatoes and simmer another 15 minutes. Remove and discard the lemongrass. Add the corn and the salmon and let the soup simmer very gently over low heat for 5 minutes. Stir in the cream and cilantro, and then add a generous pinch of salt and several turns of black pepper. Taste the soup, adjust the seasoning, and ladle into warmed soup bowls. Serve immediately.

Note: To make fish stock, place 3 pounds of fish heads and bones (without skins), 1 large quartered yellow onion, 2 or 3 sprigs Italian parsley, 1 bay leaf, $1/2$ lemon, 1 cup dry white wine, 1 teaspoon black peppercorns, and 4 cups water in a large soup kettle. Bring the mixture to a boil, reduce the heat, skim off any scum that forms, and simmer for 30 minutes. Strain the stock, cool it, and refrigerate it for up to 3 days. You may also freeze fish stock. As a substitute for true stock, use a mixture of 2 parts clam juice, 1 part white wine, 1 part water, and the juice of 1 lemon.

VARIATION:

COCONUT MILK: Instead of the heavy cream, use $3/4$ cup coconut milk.

Thai-Style Tomato Soup with Chicken, Coconut Milk, & Cilantro

Serves 4 to 6

This soup borrows several elements from Thai cuisine, including the evocative flavors of lemongrass, fish sauce, and coconut. In addition, cutting the chicken pieces through the bone is a traditional Thai technique. If you'd rather not have the bones to discard as you eat, bone the chicken before cutting it and reduce the cooking time to about 10 minutes.

1 chicken breast, bone in
2 chicken leg-thigh pieces, bone in
2 tablespoons peanut oil
2 shallots, finely minced
1/2 cup scallions, finely chopped
3 cloves garlic, minced
2 serrano peppers, minced
1 tablespoon finely minced fresh ginger
3 cups homemade chicken stock

3 stalks lemongrass, bruised and cut into 1-inch pieces
Juice of 2 limes
3 tablespoons fish sauce (Nam Pla)
2 cups fresh tomato pulp
3 cups coconut milk
3 tablespoons coconut cream
Kosher salt
1/4 cup minced fresh cilantro leaves

Divide the chicken breast into halves. Using a meat cleaver, cut the breast and leg-thigh parts through the bone into bite-size pieces (about 1 1/2 inches). Set aside. Heat the oil in a large, heavy pot and sauté the shallots until they are soft and fragrant. Add the scallions, and sauté them until they are limp, and then add the garlic, serrano peppers, and ginger and sauté another 2 minutes. Stir in the chicken stock, chicken pieces, lemongrass, lime juice, fish sauce, and tomato pulp. Bring the soup to a simmer, reduce the heat to very low, cover the pot, and simmer about 15 to 20 minutes, until the chicken is cooked through. Remove the lid and add the coconut milk and coconut cream. Stir the soup, heat it thoroughly, and then taste. Add additional lime juice, fish sauce, or salt to correct the balance of flavors. Ladle the soup into warmed bowls and top each portion with a sprinkling of cilantro leaves.

🧄 Pasta Fagioli Soup

Serves 4

There are endless variations of this traditional Italian soup, and I've never had one I didn't enjoy. I particularly like this one in fall, when the weather is turning cool but a few of summer's tomatoes linger.

2 tablespoons olive oil
1 yellow onion, diced
6 to 8 cloves garlic, minced
1 cup Tomato Essence (page 235)
2 cups concentrated duck stock (4 cups normal strength reduced to 2 cups)
2 cups water

2 cups cannellini beans, cooked
2 medium fresh tomatoes, in season
1 tablespoon fresh oregano leaves
2 teaspoons minced fresh Italian parsley
4 ounces (1 cup) small dry pasta (ditalini, tripolini)
Fresh parmigiano or Romano Pecorino cheese

Heat the olive oil in a heavy soup pot. Sauté the onions until they are limp and transparent, add the garlic, and sauté another 2 minutes. Add the tomato essence, duck stock, water, beans, fresh tomatoes, and herbs and simmer over low heat for 30 minutes. Stir in the pasta, cook until the pasta is just tender, and remove the soup from the heat. Ladle the soup into bowls and grate a tablespoon or two of cheese over the top. Serve immediately.

🧅 White Bean, Tomato, & Chorizo Soup with Cilantro

Serves 6 to 8

This hearty blend of flavors and textures is one of my favorite winter soups.

8 ounces dry white beans (Great Northerns or small whites)

3 tablespoons pure olive oil

1 yellow onion, choppped

1 pasilla pepper, seeded and cut in small julienne

1 jalapeño pepper, seeded and minced

1 pound bulk chorizo sausage

6 cloves garlic, crushed and minced

8 cups homemade chicken stock

1 28-ounce can diced tomatoes, crushed tomatoes, or whole tomatoes, chopped

$1/2$ cup cilantro leaves

Kosher salt and freshly ground black pepper

2 limes, cut in quarters

Soak the beans overnight in enough water to cover them, plus 2 inches.

Rinse and drain the beans, place them in a heavy pot, cover them with fresh water, and simmer them over medium heat for about 20 minutes, until they are almost tender. In a large heavy pot, heat the olive oil. Add the onions and, with the heat on medium, sauté them until they are fragrant and translucent, about 15 to 20 minutes. Add the peppers and sauté until they are limp, and then add the sausage and sauté for about 10 minutes, using a fork to break it into small, uniform pieces. Stir in the garlic and sauté for another 2 minutes.

Drain and rinse the white beans, and add them to the onion mixture along with the chicken stock and tomatoes. Cover the soup and simmer it over medium heat for 30 minutes. Remove the lid, stir in the cilantro leaves, and add salt and pepper to taste. Ladle the soup into warmed bowls and add a squeeze of lime to each just before serving, or place a wedge of lime alongside.

🧅 Potato Soup with Tomatoes & Peppers

Serves 4 to 6

I love almost any type of potato soup, and here I offer several variations on the same theme.

2 to 3 tablespoons pure olive oil
1 medium yellow onion
6 cloves garlic, minced
2 jalapeño or serrano peppers, minced
2 pounds small red, Yellow Finn, or Yukon gold potatoes, scrubbed and sliced
3 cups homemade chicken stock

3 cups water
1 28-ounce can whole peeled or sliced tomatoes
1/4 cup minced cilantro leaves
Kosher salt and freshly milled black pepper
Cilantro sauce (optional; see Note, page 97)

Heat the olive oil in a heavy soup pot. Add the onion and sauté over low heat until it is soft and transparent, about 20 minutes. Add the garlic an the peppers, sauté for another 2 minutes, and add the potatoes. Pour in the chicken stock and the water and simmer the mixture until the potatoes are almost tender, about 15 minutes. Add the tomatoes, simmer 10 minutes, season with salt and pepper to taste, and stir in the cilantro leaves. Top with cilantro sauce if desired. Serve the soup immediately or chill and reheat it. It will keep, refrigerated for several days.

VARIATIONS:

CREAMY POTATO-TOMATO SOUP: Purée the soup with an immersion blender and top each serving with a spoonful of Aioli (page 254)

POTATO-TOMATO-LEEK SOUP: Instead of the onion, use 3 leeks with 2 inches of green stem left on. Omit the pepper and add the juice of $1/2$ lemon to finish the soup.

SMOKY POTATO-TOMATO SOUP: Substitute 1 chipotle pepper for the jalapeño and use smoked tomatoes (page 93). Purée the soup and top with Chipotle Mayonnaise (page 255) before serving.

❀ Tomato & Crab Bisque with Ginger & Golden Caviar

This is a lush and elegant soup, ideal on New Year's Eve when crab is in season.

1 or 2 tablespoons butter
1 yellow onion, diced
1 quart homemade chicken stock
3-inch piece of fresh ginger, thinly sliced
1 whole Pacific crab, cleaned
¼ cup crème fraîche (see Note)
3 ounces golden caviar
Juice of 1 lemon

1 16-ounce can of diced tomatoes
8 ounces strained tomatoes or tomato sauce, canned
Salt and black pepper
1 teaspoon pressed fresh ginger
3 or 4 tablespoons sherry, optional
2 tablespoons fresh cilantro leaves

Melt the butter in a heavy pot. Add the onions and sauté over low heat until the onion is soft and transparent, about 20 minutes. Add the chicken stock and half of the slices of ginger and simmer over low heat for 30 minutes. While the stock is simmering, pick the crabmeat from its shell, reserving all shells. Keep the crab legs whole and refrigerate the picked meat until it is needed. Add the crab shells to the stock, cover the pot, and simmer 30 minutes.

Meanwhile, mix together the crème fraîche and a tablespoon of the caviar, along with just a squeeze (about 1 or 2 teaspoons) of lemon juice. Refrigerate. Strain the stock and return the liquid to the pot. Add all the tomatoes and the remaining ginger slices and simmer for 15 minutes. The soup can be made in advance up to this point. Let it rest until you are ready to complete it.

Strain the soup a final time, return it to the heat, and reduce it by 25 percent. Have the crab, caviar cream, and cilantro nearby. Taste the broth, season with salt and pepper, and stir in the pressed ginger for more ginger flavor. Add the sherry if you are using it. Divide the body meat of the crab among 6 soup bowls and ladle the broth over. Add 2 crab legs to each serving, top with a large tablespoon of caviar cream and a teaspoon of caviar, and finish with a scattering of cilantro leaves. Serve immediately.

🧅 Tomato Stilton Soup

This soup is rich without being heavy, and full of great depth of flavor.

4 to 6 tablespoons olive oil
2 medium leeks (about 1
    cup), white and pale
    green part, washed,
    drained, and thinly
    sliced
1 white or yellow onion,
    diced
2 tablespoons minced
    garlic
1 28-ounce can crushed
    peeled tomatoes or 4
    cups peeled, seeded,
    and diced plum
    tomatoes

4 cups homemade chicken
    stock
2 tablespoons finely
    minced fresh sage leaves
1 1/2 cups crumbled Stilton
    cheese
1 tablespoon finely
    minced fresh Italian
    parsley
Black pepper in a mill

In a heavy kettle, heat enough olive oil to generously coat the pan. Add the leeks and onion and sauté them until they are soft and fragrant, about 15 minutes. Add the garlic and cook for an additional 2 minutes. Stir in the tomatoes, broth, and sage and bring the mixture to a boil. Reduce the heat, and simmer for 15 minutes. Add the cheese and stir constantly over low heat until it is just melted. Stir in the parsley, add several turns of pepper, and serve immediately.

✿ Tomato-Eggplant Soup with Lamb Meatballs

Serves 6 to 8

The meatballs make this rich soup even heartier. If time is a consideration, you can certainly omit them and have a thoroughly delightful, filling soup.

2 medium or 3 small egg-
  plants
5 medium tomatoes, peeled
Pure olive oil
1 large onion, finely
  chopped
6 cloves garlic, minced
2 bay leaves, crushed
Pinch of marjoram
2$^{1}/_{2}$ quarts duck or beef
  stock
2 teaspoons minced onion
$^{3}/_{4}$ pound ground lamb

2 teaspoons finely minced
  lemon zest
$^{1}/_{2}$ teaspoon finely minced
  fresh oregano
Kosher salt and freshly
  milled black pepper
2 ounces (about $^{1}/_{2}$ cup)
  feta cheese, cut in $^{1}/_{4}$-
  inch cubes
Flour
1 tablespoon snipped
  chives

Over a flame or in a 350°F oven, roast the eggplants until they are very soft. If roasting the eggplants over a flame, turn each one as its skin darkens, continuing until the egg-plant is soft and rather limp. Depending on the size and ripeness of the eggplant and the intensity of the flame, it can take up to 25 minutes. Roasting the eggplants in the oven takes from 25 to 45 minutes.

Place the tomatoes in a heavy skillet or roasting pan, toss with a small amount of olive oil, and roast in the oven until they are soft, fragrant and almost browned. Set both the eggplants and the tomatoes aside to cool.

Meanwhile, in a large, heavy pot sauté the chopped onion in olive oil until it is soft and fragrant. Add about two-thirds of the garlic, reserving the rest for the meatballs. Sauté another 2 minutes, and add the bay and marjoram. Remove from the heat. When the eggplants are cool enough to handle, peel and chop them and add them to the onion mixture. Press the tomatoes through a sieve, discard the seeds, and add the juice and pulp to the onion and eggplant. Stir in the stock and simmer the soup, covered, for 30 minutes. Purée the soup with an immersion blender or, for a smoother texture, strain it through a sieve.

Sauté the reserved garlic and the minced onion in a small amount of olive oil for 4 or 5 minutes. In a small mixing bowl, combine the ground lamb, sautéed garlic and onion, 1 teaspoon of the lemon zest, the oregano, a generous pinch of salt, and several turns of pepper. When the mixture is well combined, add the feta cheese and mix quickly and lightly. Form tiny meatballs, roll them in flour, and brown them in a heavy skillet. Bring the soup to a boil, lower the heat, add the meatballs, and simmer 10 minutes. Serve immediately, garnished with the remaining lemon zest and the chives.

Pork & Dried-Corn Stew with Tomatoes, Roasted Garlic, & Chilies

Serves 6 to 8

As the foods and recipes of the American Southwest have grown in popularity, posole has become a more common ingredient than it once was. The word posole itself refers both to white field corn and to the celebratory stews in which it plays a major role. Dried posole takes several hours of cooking to become tender, but frozen posole requires just a couple of hours, which is still more time than many of us have except on rare occasions. Although posole somewhat resembles canned hominy, substituting it will yield vastly different results than you will achieve with the real thing. Both dried and fresh-frozen posole are available in specialty stores and by mail order.

2 quarts homemade chicken or duck stock, plus extra for cooking posole

2 pounds pork shoulder

3 cups dried or frozen posole

3 tablespoons pure olive oil

1 yellow onion

8 cloves garlic

2 serrano peppers

4 pasilla peppers

1 tablespoon cumin

8 ounces tomato sauce

4 cups fresh tomato pulp or canned diced tomatoes

$1/4$ cup roasted-garlic purée (see Note)

1 tablespoon minced Mexican oregano leaves

Salt and black pepper

¹/₄ cup fresh chopped	¹/₄ cabbage, shredded
cilantro leaves	Commercial hot sauce
2 limes, cut in wedges	

Cut half of the pork into small cubes. Brown it in a large heavy skillet and add 1 cup of stock. Simmer over medium heat until the stock has nearly evaporated. Repeat this process 3 times. Add the remaining quart of stock, cover the pot, and simmer over low heat for 20 minutes. Remove from the heat, strain the stock, and discard the pork. This can be done a day or two in advance. Refrigerate the stock until ready to use.

Several hours before you are ready to complete the soup, prepare the *posole*, rinsing it first under cool water if you are using the dried variety. Place the *posole* in a large, heavy pot and cover it with plenty of stock or fresh water. Cook dried *posole*, for 3 hours; frozen, 1 hour. Drain the *posole*.

Heat the olive oil in a large, heavy pot and sauté the onion until it is tender and fragrant. Add the garlic and the chilies, sauté 2 minutes, and stir in the cumin. Cut the remaining pork into 1¹/₂-inch slices, add it to the onion mixture, and brown. Pour the stock over the meat and vegetables and bring it to a simmer. Add the *posole*, lower the heat, cover the pot, and simmer over very low heat for 2 hours. Remove the lid, add the tomato sauce, tomatoes, roasted garlic, and oregano and simmer for another half hour. Taste the stew and add salt and pepper as needed. Remove from the heat and ladle the stew into hot bowls. Top each serving with a sprinkling of cilantro leaves, a squeeze of lime, and a handful of shredded cabbage. Pass the hot sauce.

Note: To make roasted garlic purée, clean 2 or 3 heads of raw garlic, leaving the bulb intact but removing any dirt that may cling to the roots and as much of the dry outer skin as will come off easily. Place the bulbs in a small ovenproof dish or pan, add about $1/2$ cup olive oil and $1/4$ cup water, season with salt and pepper, cover, and bake at 325°F for 45 to 60 minutes, until the garlic is the consistency of soft butter. Remove the garlic from the oven and let it cool on absorbent paper. When it is cool enough to be handled easily, set the garlic on a cutting board, remove the root, and use the heel of your hand to press out the garlic pump. If necessary, squeeze the pulp out clove by clove. Scrape the pulp off the cutting board, place it in a small bowl, and mash it with a fork until it is smooth. A head of garlic will yield approximately 2 tablespoons of purée.

 Tomato Toast

Serves 2 to 4

This is one of the simplest versions of toasted bread and tomatoes.

4 thick slices of sour-
  dough or other country-
  style bread
2 large cloves garlic,
  peeled and cut in half

2 small ripe red tomatoes
  (stupice are perfect),
  cut in half
Kosher salt and freshly
  ground black pepper

Toast or grill the bread until it is golden. Rub each slice with the cut side of a half clove of garlic, using a fresh piece of garlic every time. Rub each slice with half of a tomato, pressing firmly to push the pulp into the bread. Discard the skins and remaining pulp. Add a little salt and pepper to each slice of bread and serve immediately.

🕷️ Savory Scones with Dried Tomatoes, Dry Jack Cheese, & Fresh Sage

Makes 8 to 12 scones

These light and fragrant scones are perfect for brunch.

³/₄ cup whole milk or half-and-half
¹/₄ cup dried-tomato bits
2 cups flour
1 tablespoon baking powder
¹/₂ teaspoon salt
5 tablespoons butter, chilled and cut into ¹/₄-inch pieces

1 egg, beaten
2 tablespoons minced fresh sage leaves
³/₄ cup grated Dry Jack cheese
12 perfect sage leaves
Heavy cream

Place a baking sheet in the oven and preheat to 450°F.

In a small bowl, pour the milk over the dried-tomato bits and let sit for 30 minutes. Mix together the flour, baking powder, and salt. Add the butter and, using either your fingertips or a pastry blender, quickly work it into the flour mixture so that it has the consistency of bread crumbs. Stir the egg and sage into the milk and dried tomatoes. Make a well in the center of the flour mixture, pour the milk in, and mix lightly and quickly with a fork until it forms a loose, soft dough. Add the cheese, blend quickly with your fingers, and turn the dough out onto a lightly floured surface. Knead very softly for 30 seconds.

Using a rolling pin or patting with the palm of your hand, spread out the dough into a rectangle ³/₄ inch thick. Using a sharp knife, cut into 8 to 12 triangles. Brush the surface of each scone with the heavy cream and then very lightly press a sage leaf into the center of each scone. Brush with a little more cream if necessary to make the leaf stay in place.

Using a spatula, transfer the scones to the hot baking sheet and bake until lightly golden, about 10 minutes. Remove them from the oven and transfer them immediately to a cooling rack. Serve with Dried-Tomato Butter (page 251), Tomato Butter (page 250), or Spicy Tomato Jelly (page 274).

Popovers with Dried Tomatoes

Makes about 1 dozen popovers

A popover rising all golden and fragrant out of its tin is a cozy, pleasing sight, and one that is extremely welcome on a cold morning. If you like a bit of something sweet for breakfast, serve these delicate little clouds with Spicy Tomato Jelly (page 274).

1 ¹/₃ cups milk, room
   temperature
1 tablespoon melted butter
1 ¹/₃ cups all-purpose flour
¹/₃ cup sun-dried tomato
   bits
1 tablespoon finely minced
   fresh Italian parsley

¹/₂ teaspoon kosher salt
3 eggs, room temperature
³/₄ cup Fontina cheese
Dried-Tomato Butter
   or Tomato Butter
   (optional, pages 251
   and 250)

Have heavy, deep muffin tins (cast iron works best) buttered and ready, with the oven preheated to 450°F. Heat the milk and butter together over medium heat. When the butter is melted, add the flour, tomato bits, parsley, and salt, and beat vigorously with a wooden spoon until the mixture comes together and pulls away from the side of the pan. Remove from the heat immediately. Add the eggs, one at a time, beating well after each addition but not overbeating.

Spoon just enough of the popover batter into each muffin tin to completely coat the bottom. Divide the cheese among the 12 popovers and then fill each tin about one-half to two-thirds full with the remaining batter. Bake immediately and after 15 minutes reduce the heat to 325°F. Bake for another 15 to 30 minutes until the outsides of the popovers are firm and the tops golden. Remove them from the oven and serve them immediately, with a tomato butter on the side if desired.

THE MAKING OF A SANDWICH

Who invented the sandwich? Although the discovery is credited to the fourth Earl of Sandwich (1718–1792), I suspect that it was much earlier than the earl's legendary evenings at the gambling table that a man or a woman first folded a savory ingredient or two between a couple of slices of bread. The naming of the concoction, that's a matter for the early marketers, and someone apparently sensed the catchy appeal of the earl's district.

Regardless of its origins, the sandwich is firmly entrenched in the culinary practices of numerous cultures, none more so perhaps than here in the United States, where it remains in its diverse forms the single most common lunch item. And a slice or two of tomato graces the majority of our sandwiches year round, regardless of the season. Fast-food hamburgers automatically come with tomatoes unless you request otherwise. Then, of course, there's turkey on whole wheat with *lettuce-and-tomato*: so essential, and with its ingredients so linked together they are nearly a single item. This ubiquitous form is not, however, the best use of the tomato between two slices of bread. For the sandwich's finest moment, one needs to look to summer, to gardens full of sun-warmed tomatoes, and to the best bread you can find.

One could say that summer *is* a tomato sandwich. The essence of all that is good about the leisurely season is distilled in the simple, compelling combination of bread, tomato, and salt. The silky texture, like liquid sunlight; the sweetness and the slight burst of acidity; the way the juices sink down into the bread. At no other time of year is this elemental pleasure ours except in the languid days of summer's heat. Don't let summer pass without having your fill of its simplest pleasure.

Americans love sandwiches, in part because we tend to eat on the go—in the car or on foot or whatever mode of transportation—nearly anywhere that it is not forbidden. Although it is not my favorite way of dining—I prefer a stationary rather than a mobile meal—I thoroughly appreciate a great sandwich, especially one that involves summer tomatoes.

These variations on one of our country's favorite culinary themes builds on the concept of the simple summer tomato sandwich in a variety of delicious ways. Do keep in mind that a sandwich will not be better than the bread it is built upon. Use the best available to you, and if that's not good enough, make your own. Few things are as pleasantly therapeutic as the baking of bread.

❀ Summer Tomato Sandwiches, Version 1

Serves 1, easily increased

Invariably, I make this sandwich immediately upon the discovery of the first tomatoes of the season. I never grow tired of it, and think of it longing as I await the first of the harvest.

Homemade or best-quality commercial mayonnaise
2 slices of your favorite bread (I prefer thick, coarse Italian bread)

1 medium garden tomato, stem end removed, sliced $1/4$ inch thick
Kosher salt

Spread a liberal amount of mayonnaise over both pieces of bread. Place the slices of tomato on top of the mayonnaise, and sprinkle them with salt. Put the two slices of bread together or, better yet, leave open-faced.

❧ Summer Tomato Sandwiches, Version 2

Serves 4

This one's only slightly more complex than a simple tomato sandwich, and it's bright with the flavors of sweet basil and onions, two of summer's other delights.

8 slices of thick, country-style bread
Homemade or best-quality commerical mayonnaise
4 garden tomatoes, stem end removed, sliced 1/4 inch thick

1 medium or two small sweet onions, peeled and cut in thin rounds
Several leaves of fresh basil
Kosher salt and freshly ground black pepper

Toast the bread. Spread a liberal amount of mayonnaise over each slice. Top 4 slices of bread with several slices of tomato followed by rounds of onion, a few basil leaves, and sprinkles of salt and pepper. Top with the remaining slices of bread.

🧅 Summer Tomato Sandwiches, Version 3

Makes 4 sandwiches

I prefer this sandwich on whole-wheat sourdough bread or, when I can find them, on whole-wheat sourdough sausage buns, which are the perfect shape for nestling all the ingredients. If these breads are not available, your favorite will do.

4 whole-wheat sourdough sausage rolls, or enough other bread for 4 sandwiches
2 large or 3 medium garden tomatoes, stem ends removed and sliced
2 medium lemon cucumbers or 1 medium green cucumber (see Note), unpeeled and thinly sliced
1 red onion, thinly sliced
Garlic, very finely minced
Extra-virgin olive oil
Kosher salt and freshly ground black pepper
Fresh basil leaves

Open the sausage rolls or set 4 slices of bread on your work surface. Divide the tomato slices among them, and follow with the cucumber and onion slices. Sprinkle the garlic and drizzle about a tablespoon of olive oil over the surface of the vegetables. Season with salt and pepper, and top with 3 or 4 basil leaves. If using 4 bread slices, cap them with the remaining slices. Serve immediately.

VARIATION:

SALAMI: Add several slices of Italian salami or soppresatta to each sandwich before the tomatoes.

Note: Commercial green cucumbers should always be peeled because they are generally waxed before being shipped to market. Those from your garden or purchased at farm markets do not require peeling.

Roasted-Tomato Sandwich

Makes 4 sandwiches

If you have plenty of garden tomatoes, I recommend keeping several roasted ones on hand in the refrigerator during the peak of the season. They're perfect for a quick meal and great turned into a fast sauce. Here, they create one of the simplest sandwiches imaginable and it's a real treat—bright, refreshing, and full of the essence of summer. It is, by the way, a rather messy sandwich, so be prepared for lots of dripping and oozing out the sides. If such a mess does not appeal to you, simply serve the sandwiches open-faced.

4 large or 8 medium
   garden tomatoes, ripe
   or very ripe
1 tablespoon extra-virgin
   olive oil
3 cloves garlic

1 fresh sourdough ba-
   guette, cut into four
   pieces, each split in half
Kosher salt and freshly
   ground black pepper
Handful of basil leaves,
   thinly sliced, or 2 tablespoons snipped chives

Roast the tomatoes several hours before using so that they have time to cool and chill. Peel the tomatoes, cut off the stem ends, and place them in a shallow baking dish. Drizzle the olive oil over the tomatoes and turn them to coat them in the oil. Bake them in a 325°F oven until they are very soft and beginning to brown, from 40 to 60 minutes. Drain off the juices (reserve them for soup, stock, or salad dressing) every 20 minutes so that the tomatoes roast nearly dry rather than stew in their juices. Remove them from the oven, allow them to cool, and then refrigerate until ready to use.

To assemble the sandwiches, toast, grill, or broil both sides of the baguette slices until golden and slightly crisp. Place several spoonsful of the tomato pulp onto the lower pieces of the baguette, top with a sprinkling of salt and pepper, add the other piece of the baguette to each portion. Serve immediately.

VARIATIONS:

GARLIC: Before roasting, top each tomato with a teaspoon of finely minced fresh garlic.

SPICY: Add 1 or 2 jalapeños or serranos, stemmed, cut open, and seeded, to the tomatoes before roasting. Chop the peppers and store them with the tomatoes. When assembling the sandwiches, add a sprinkling of fresh cilantro leaves as a final topping.

SMOKED: Replace the roasted tomatoes with smoked tomatoes (page 236).

The bacon-lettuce-and-tomato sandwich is, to my palate, one of the best American culinary inventions, far better than the ubiquitous hamburger and nearly as popular. There are times when its particular combinations of flavors and textures just taste *right*, like the best thing you could ever eat: the play of salt and acid, the silky feel of a summer tomato against the salty crunch of bacon, the crisp watery crunch of the lettuce, the deep juicy mingling of mayonnaise and tomato drippings—sheer delight. Although you can get a BLT in almost any American coffee shop year-round, you know what my advice is: wait until tomato season and then enjoy it at its best.

 ## The Traditional BLT

Serves 2

Good old-fashioned white bread is best, but whatever you prefer is just fine for this American classic, as long as you use great-tasting tomatoes. Some people like to first toast the bread; if you are one of them, by all means do so.

6 slices of bacon	4 slices bread
2 ripe tomatoes	Kosher salt
1/4 cup homemade or best-quality commercial mayonnaise	Handful lettuce or other salad greens of choice

130

Fry the bacon in a heavy skillet until crisp. While it is frying, cut the tomatoes in $1/4$-inch slices. Transfer the bacon from the skillet to absorbent paper. Spread mayonnaise over each slice of bread and top 2 of the slices with enough rounds of tomato to cover the surface. Sprinkle the tomatoes with a little salt. Divide the bacon between the 2 slices of bread, add the lettuce, and then place the remaining slices of bread on top of the lettuce, mayonnaise side down, of course. Cut the sandwiches in half and serve immediately.

 The BLT Extraordinaire

Serves 4

This version is best on sourdough or other crusty bread.

$1/3$ **pound thinly sliced pancetta**	**4 ripe tomatoes, sliced**
	Salt
$1/2$ **loaf sourdough bread**	**1 bunch of arugula**
Aioli (page 254)	

Sauté the pancetta until just crisp. While it is cooking, cut the bread into $1/2$-inch slices for a total of 8 slices. Spread aioli over each piece. Arrange the tomato slices on 4 of the pieces of bread and add a sprinkling of salt. Divide the pancetta among the 4 sandwiches, placing it on top of the tomatoes. Scatter a handful of arugula on top of the pancetta and cap with the remaining slices of bread, aioli side down, of course. Cut in half and serve immediately.

 # The California BLT

Serves 4

This sandwich evokes the traditional version while adding an additional dimension with the mustard and avocado. Not for the purist, perhaps, but absolutely wonderful.

^{1}/$_3$ pound sliced apple-
   smoked bacon
^{1}/$_2$ loaf sourdough bread
Dijon mustard
1 medium-ripe avocado,
   peeled and sliced

4 ripe tomatoes, sliced
Salt and pepper
About 1 ^{1}/$_2$ cups mustard
   sprouts or onion sprouts

Sauté the bacon until just crisp. While it is cooking, cut the bread into ^{1}/$_2$-inch slices for a total of 8 slices. Toast or grill the bread lightly. Spread a teaspoon or two of mustard over each slice of bread. Divide the avocado among 4 slices of bread and top it with the tomatoes. Sprinkle the tomatoes with a little salt and pepper, and top them with the bacon, a small handful of sprouts, and the remaining slices of bread. Cut in half and serve immediately.

 # The Pacific BLT

Serves 4

When I want a hearty but rustic lunch, this is one of my favorites. I love the combination of textures and the extra kick provided by the chipotle peppers in the mayonnaise.

1/3 pound sliced apple-smoked bacon

4 fish fillets, about 3 to 4 ounces each (snapper, catfish, or rock cod)

1 egg, beaten

3/4 cup fresh bread crumbs, toasted

Chipotle Mayonnaise (page 255)

4 sourdough rolls, split

4 ripe tomatoes, sliced

1 small red onion, peeled and cut in thin rounds

Sauté the bacon until just crisp. While it is cooking, dredge the fish fillets first in the egg and then in the bread crumbs. Remove the bacon from the frying pan and let it drain on absorbent paper. Fry the fish in the bacon drippings, turning once, until both sides are golden brown. Drain well on absorbent paper. Spread a teaspoon of two of the mayonnaise on the inside of each roll and top it with slices of tomato, followed by bacon, then onion rounds, then fish. If you want, top each fish fillet with a little more of the mayonnaise. Serve immediately.

 Grilled Skirt Steak with Tomato-Onion Relish

Serves 4

This sandwich is messy and luscious, the perfect lunch on a cold winter day.

1 pound skirt steak	Kosher salt and freshly
¹/₂ cup balsamic vinegar	ground black pepper
¹/₂ cup pure olive oil	4 sourdough French rolls
3 cloves garlic, crushed	Tomato-Onion Relish
1 tablespoon minced fresh	(page 275)
ginger	

Cut the skirt steak, with the grain, in 4 equal strips and place them in a low glass or stainless-steel pan or bowl. Combine the vinegar, olive oil, garlic, and ginger and pour the mixture over the strips of steak. Season with salt and pepper and let rest for at least 30 minutes or up to 3 hours. Refrigerate the steak if you want to marinate it for more than 30 minutes.

Remove the steak from the marinade and grill or sauté each strip for about 2 or 3 minutes on each side, so that the meat is cooked but still rare and juicy. Toast the rolls and let the steak rest a minute or two on your work surface, and then slice it, with the grain, in thin strips. Open each roll on your work surface and spread the relish over the bottom pieces. Top the relish with the portions of sliced skirt steak and serve the sandwiches immediately.

 *Tomato Bread Pudding*

Serves 6

Just another variation on the ever-popular sandwich theme, this version of savory bread pudding is a sort of baked BLT custard.

Pure olive oil
1/2 pound bacon or pancetta
4 cups hearty peasant bread, torn into medium-sized chunks
2 medium-sized ripe slicing tomatoes
3 tablespoons finely minced fresh Italian parsley

2 ounces Gruyère, Fontina, or St. George cheese, grated
2 eggs, beaten
2 1/4 cups milk
2 tablespoons puréed sun-dried tomatoes
2 cloves garlic, finely minced or pressed
Kosher salt and freshly ground black pepper
1 quart fresh salad greens

Rub a small (1 1/2-quart) baking dish with a thin coating of olive oil. Fry the bacon or pancetta until it is *almost* crisp. Have the bread ready in a large mixing bowl. Transfer the bacon to absorbent paper, let the pan drippings cool briefly, and then pour them over the bread and toss together well. Add the tomatoes, parsley, and cheese and toss again. Crumble the bacon, add it to the bread and tomato mixture, and toss lightly. Transfer the mixture to the baking dish. Whisk together the eggs, milk, tomato purée, and garlic. Season with a generous pinch of salt and several turns of black pepper. Pour the custard over the bread and agitate the dish so that it distributes evenly.

Bake the bread pudding in a 325°F oven for about 35 minutes, then increase the heat to 425° and bake for an additional 10 to 15 minutes, until the top of the pudding is lightly and evenly browned. Remove from the oven and let rest at least 10 minutes before serving alongside the salad greens.

🕷 Dried-Tomato Quiche with Chèvre Crust

Serves 6 to 8

Although we pay more and more attention to the amount of saturated fat in our diets, quiche has remained quite popular. I do not make it often, but enjoy it occasionally, with a big green salad alongside.

1 1/4 cups all-purpose flour
1 teaspoon kosher salt
3 tablespoons butter
3 ounces chèvre
1/4 cup dried-tomato bits
1/4 cup dry white wine
Pure olive oil
1 yellow onion, diced
4 cloves garlic, minced

1 small eggplant, peeled and cut in 3/4-inch cubes
Kosher salt and freshly ground black pepper
1/4 cup minced fresh herbs (chives, oregano, marjoram, thyme, basil)
1 cup grated cheese (Asiago, Fontina, or Gruyère)

3 eggs	2 tablespoons roasted-
2 cups half-and-half or	garlic purée (page 118)
cream	8 marinated dried-tomato
	halves

Mix together the flour and salt and place it in a food processor. Add the butter and chèvre and pulse several times, until the dough just comes together. Transfer the mixture to a floured surface, gather it up into a ball, and chill it for 1 hour. Roll it out to fit a 9-inch springform pan and press it into the pan. Weight the surface and bake the shell in a 400°F oven for about 12 minutes, until the pastry just begins to turn golden.

Meanwhile, combine the dried-tomato bits and white wine in a small bowl and let sit for 30 minutes. Heat a small amount of olive oil in a heavy skillet, add the onion, and sauté until it is soft and fragrant, about 15 minutes. Add the garlic, sauté an additional 2 minutes, and then add the eggplant. Reduce the heat and cook the eggplant until it is very soft and tender. Add the wine and dried-tomato mixture, stir, and remove from the heat. Let cool slightly, taste, season with salt and pepper, and then toss with the fresh herbs.

Spread the vegetable mixture over the surface of the baked pie shell and top with the grated cheese. Mix together the eggs, half-and-half, and roasted-garlic purée. Pour the custard over the vegetables and bake at 375°F for about 35 to 40 minutes, being sure not to overcook. Remove from the oven and cool for at least 20 minutes. Garnish each serving with a piece of marinated dried tomato.

FOCACCIA

Focaccia is one of the best vehicles for enjoying the flavor of tomatoes year-round. In the summertime, make a simple focaccia, cut it in single serving portions, and top each serving with fresh tomatoes and other vegetables and herbs from the garden. When tomatoes are out of season, brush the fococcia before baking with a savory tomato sauce and top it with green onions, which will become tender and fragrant in the oven. Use focaccia to make sandwiches year-round.

My focaccia recipe is a variation of one of Carol Field's recipes in *The Italian Baker*, altered for the quantity I find most convenient at home and adjusted for coarse-grain kosher salt rather than fine-grain sea salt.

🧅 *Basic Focaccia Dough*

Makes 1 12- by 17-inch rectangular bread

Your dough will rise most effectively if it rests in a slightly warm area, but do not set it too close to a direct source of heat. My house is frequently quite cold in the winter months, and I use a heating pad covered with several layers of towels to diffuse the heat. In a normally warm room, you will not need to make special arrangements.

2 $^1/_2$ teaspoons dry yeast
$^1/_4$ cup warm water
1 $^1/_2$ tablespoons fragrant extra-virgin olive oil, plus about 4 tablespoons for baking

1 $^1/_4$ cups plus 1 or 2 tablespoons water, room temperature
4 $^1/_4$ cups unbleached all-purpose flour
1 tablespoon kosher salt

Place the yeast and warm water in the bowl of your mixer and let stand until the yeast is creamy. Add the olive oil and 1 cup water and stir the mixture with the paddle. Add the flour and all but $^1/_2$ teaspoon salt and mix on low until the dough comes together, adding more water if necessary. Change to the dough hook and knead on low speed for 2 minutes; change to high and knead an additional 2 or 3 minutes, until the dough is smooth and velvety. Transfer the dough to a bowl oiled with olive oil, cover it tightly with plastic wrap, and place it in a slightly warm—but not hot—area until it has doubled, about 1 $^1/_2$ hours.

When the dough has doubled, shape it to fit into an oiled half-sheet pan. Cover it with a tea towel, let it rise for 30 minutes, and then dimple the dough, using your fingertips to make half-inch impressions over the entire surface.

Cover with a moist tea towel and let rise until doubled again, about 2 hours.

For basic focaccia, brush the surface of the dough with a generous 3 or 4 tablespoons of extra-virgin olive oil and then sprinkle with the reserved salt.

Bake the focaccia in a 400°F oven for 15 to 20 minutes. Spray the focaccia with water 3 times during the first 10 minutes of cooking. When the focaccia is done, remove it from the oven, and transfer it to a rack immediately. Let it cool and serve it at room temperature.

VARIATIONS:

TOMATO SAUCE: Mix 2 tablespoons of extra-virgin olive oil with 6 tablespoons tomato sauce and spread the mixture over the dough, in place of the plain olive oil, before baking. Sprinkle it with several turns of black pepper and 1 teaspoon kosher salt before placing it in the oven.

GREEN ONIONS: After topping the focaccia with the tomato sauce and olive oil mixture as in the preceding variation, spread 1/2 cup thinly sliced rounds of green onion over it all. Add salt and pepper and bake.

TOMATO CONCASSÉ: Combine 2 tablespoons of extra-virgin olive oil with 1/2 cup Tomato Concassé (page 231) and spread the mixture over the focaccia before baking. Season with salt and pepper. Before serving, top each piece with a sprinkling of minced fresh herbs or a leaf or two of basil.

SUN-DRIED TOMATOES: Mix 2 tablespoons of extra-virgin olive oil with 2 tablespoons puréed sun-dried tomatoes (the type in a tube works perfectly here), 1 tablespoon warm water, and 1 teaspoon chopped fresh thyme leaves and spread the combination over the dough before baking.

❧ Focaccia with Cherry Tomatoes

Serves 4 to 6

This makes a great lunch in August or September, when cherry tomatoes are abundant. It is a simple rustic dish, somewhere between a salad and a sandwich and very, very good. If you have day-old focaccia on hand, warm it in a 325°F oven for 10 minutes before assembling.

1 recipe Basic Focaccia
   Dough (preceding
   recipe)
4 cups small tomatoes
   (such as cherry or pear),
   sliced in half

2 tablespoons extra-virgin
   olive oil
Kosher salt and freshly
   ground black pepper
Several basil leaves, cut in
   thin strips

Cut the focaccia into single servings and place them on a large platter or on individual plates. Toss the tomatoes with the olive oil and season with salt and pepper. Top each slice of focaccia with about ³/₄ cup of the tomatoes and garnish with several strips of basil. Serve immediately.

VARIATION:
Sprinkle about 1 teaspoon balsamic vinegar over the tomatoes just before serving.

🧅 Focaccia with Summer Tomatoes

Makes 8 servings

This version makes use of the flavor of ripe garden tomatoes. If you don't like anchovies, simply omit them.

1 recipe Basic Focaccia
   Dough (page 139)
3 medium garden tomatoes
2 cloves garlic, crushed
   and minced
2 tablespoons extra-virgin
   olive oil

4 to 6 anchovies, soaked
   in two tablespoons red
   wine vinegar
2 teaspoons minced fresh
   herbs
Kosher salt and freshly
   ground black pepper

Cut the focaccia into 8 pieces and place them on individual serving plates. Remove the ends of the tomatoes and cut them into 1/4-inch slices. Cover each piece of focaccia with several slices of tomato. Combine the garlic and olive oil and drizzle a bit of the mixture on each serving. Cut the anchovies in half and divide them between the servings. Drizzle each portion with a little of the anchovie's vinegar. Sprinkle each serving with fresh herbs, salt, and pepper. Serve immediately.

✿ Focaccia Sandwich with Tuna Mayonnaise, Eggs, & Tomatoes

Makes 4 large sandwiches

The technique you use for mixing the tuna and olive oil—either in a processor or by hand—will have an important impact on your final result. If you prefer a coarser, more rustic effect, mix by hand. For a smooth, more delicate taste and texture, use a processor. This sandwich, as well as the two that follow, makes great picnic fare. Be sure to wrap each sandwich tightly in plastic wrap and keep it chilled. A bowl of salt- or oil-cured olives is a perfect accompaniment to this hearty, flavorful sandwich.

1 can (6$^1/_2$ ounces) canned tuna, packed in water (see Note)
2 cloves garlic, crushed and minced
$^1/_2$ cup extra-virgin olive oil, plus up to $^1/_4$ cup

Kosher salt and freshly ground black pepper
1 recipe Basic Focaccia Dough (page 139)
2 garden tomatoes, ends removed, sliced $^1/_4$ inch thick
2 hard-boiled eggs, sliced

In a food processor or by hand, beat together the tuna, garlic, and olive oil until a thick, mayonnaise-like sauce forms. Add additional olive oil, up to $^1/_4$ cup more, if necessary to reach the desired consistency; this occurs more frequently when mixing by hand. Taste and season with salt and pepper. You can make the mayonnaise a day or two in advance, and store it in the refrigerator, covered, until ready to use.

Cut the focaccia into 8 equal pieces and spread a generous amount of the mayonnaise on 4 of them. Top with several slices of tomato and then of egg. Season with a pinch of salt and pepper. Top with the remaining pieces of bread. Serve immediately or wrap and refrigerater until ready to serve.

Note: Certainly, the best-tasting canned tuna is that imported from Italy—flavorful, dark belly meat packed in olive oil. Use it for outstanding results. But for less fat and less cost, recipes that add additional olive oil work quite well with domestic tuna packed in spring water.

❦ Focaccia Sandwich Niçoise

Makes 4 sandwiches

This is one of my favorite picnic items, and I particularly like it when it has been made several hours earlier and the flavors have had time to mingle.

8 anchovy fillets, 4 of them soaked in 1 tablespoon of red wine vinegar
1 can (6 1/2 ounces) tuna, packed in spring water, drained

3 large cloves garlic, peeled
1 tablespoon minced fresh Italian parsley
1 cup Kalamata olives, pitted (use California black olives for a milder version)

½ cup extra-virgin olive
  oil
½ cup mayonnaise
Basic Focaccia Dough
  (page 139)
Several small Red Bliss
  potatoes, steamed and
  sliced

2 hard-boiled eggs, sliced
2 garden tomatoes, ends
  removed, sliced ¼ inch
  thick
Kosher salt and freshly
  ground pepper
1 cup shredded red
  cabbage

Place 4 of the anchovy fillets (reserve the vinegared ones), tuna, garlic, parsley, and olives in a food processor. Blend the mixture until it is smooth and, with the motor still running, drizzle in the olive oil. Transfer the tapenade to a mixing bowl and fold in the mayonnaise. This portion of the recipe can be made a day or two in advance. Refrigerate the tapenade mayonnaise until ready to use.

Drain the vinegared anchovies. Cut the focaccia into 8 equal pieces and spread a generous amount of the tapenade mayonnaise over 4 of them. To these 4 slices add slices of potato, slices of egg, slices of tomato, and 1 anchovy fillet. Season with a pinch of salt and a few turns of black pepper and top with a handful of red cabbage. Brush the remaining pieces of focaccia with a small amount of the tapenade mayonnaise and place them, mayonnaise side down, on top of the cabbage. Serve immediately or wrap and chill until ready to serve.

PIZZA IN AMERICA

I have never been fond of American-style pizza, invariably slathered with a thick, cloying sauce made primarily of tomato paste, cheap red wine, and dried herbs. When I ran a small pizza pub in a college town in Northern California, we made scores of such pizzas each night, frequently responding to requests for "extra sauce." At the same time, I developed a selection of specialty pizzas, all of which used olive oil rather than tomato sauce to moisten the crust. These pizzas—especially a light and delicate one made with freshly grated zucchini, garlic, jalapeño peppers, and cheese, and topped with slices of avocado when it came out of the oven—became enormously popular, as many customers came to enjoy the way the flavors of the individual ingredients would stand out when the tomato sauce was omitted. When I want the flavor of tomatoes on pizza, I use fresh ones, which are delightful in this context. If you prefer your pizza with sauce, you can do much better than the commercial ones available. Try smoked tomato sauce (page 236) or a light Tomato Concassé (page 231) in place of thicker sauces based on commercial tomato paste; I think you will be quite pleased with the results.

🧅 Pizza and Calzone Dough

Makes 2 10- to 12-inch pizzas
or 4 small to medium calzones

Making fresh pizza dough, just like making fresh bread, requires little actual hands-on time, making it a much easier and quicker task than many people assume. And the slow rhythmic kneading of dough is such an entirely rewarding process that it's a shame more of us don't allow ourselves the time to indulge in this pleasure.

1 package or 1 tablespoon yeast	4 1/2 cups all-purpose flour
1 1/4 cups warm water	2 tablespoons extra-virgin olive oil
1 teaspoon salt	

Place the yeast and 1/4 cup of the warm water in a mixing bowl and set aside for 10 minutes. Stir in the remaining water and 1 cup of the flour. Add the salt and olive oil and stir the mixture. Add the remaining flour, cup by cup, mixing each addition completely before adding the next until you have just 1/2 cup of flour left. Turn the dough out onto a floured surface and knead until smooth and velvety, about 7 minutes, working in as much of the remaining flour as the dough will take. Place the dough in a clean bowl that has been well coated with olive oil. Cover it with a damp towel, set it in a warm place, and let it rise for 2 hours. Punch it down, let it rest for 5 minutes, and form it into the desired shape.

Pizza Margherita

Makes 2 10- to 12-inch pizzas

This classic pizza from Naples sports the colors of the Italian flag: to-mato red, basil green, and the silky white of melted cheese. The pizza is named for Queen Margherita, who presided over Italy after unification and development of the tricolored flag. Made with the finest ingredients, this simple pizza is thoroughly wonderful, one of my favorites.

1 recipe pizza dough
6 tablespoons extra-virgin
  olive oil
8 ounces mozzarella
  cheese, sliced

Handful whole fresh basil
  leaves
4 to 6 medium ripe Roma
  tomatoes, cut in rounds
Kosher salt and black
  pepper

Roll out the dough into 2 pizza skins and drizzle olive oil over each surface, followed by the mozzarella. Top the cheese with basil leaves, reserving a few for garnish, and cover it with the tomatoes. Bake the pizzas in a 500°F oven for about 15 minutes, until the crust has begun to turn golden. Remove from the oven, let rest 2 or 3 minutes, and cut into wedges. Garnish each slice with a fresh basil leaf and serve with salt and pepper alongside.

✿ Calzone with Garlic, Roasted Peppers, & Chèvre

Serves 4

This stuffed pizza is rich and satisfying, with the flavor of the roasted peppers blending beautifully with the bright taste of the tomato concassé.

3 cups roasted red
  peppers, cut in julienne
  (see Note)
1/4 cup thinly sliced fresh
  garlic
2 tablespoons balsamic
  vinegar
8 ounces young chèvre
  (such as chabis)
4 ounces aged chèvre
  (such as taupinière)

6 tablespoons fresh
  minced herbs (Italian
  parsley, chives, oregano,
  basil, thyme, marjoram)
2 teaspoons freshly
  ground black pepper
1 recipe Pizza and
  Calzone Dough (page
  147), rolled into 4
  8-inch rounds
Extra-virgin olive oil
Tomato Concassé (page
  231)

Toss together the peppers, garlic, and balsamic vinegar and set them aside. Crumble together the two chèvres and toss them with the herbs and the black pepper.

Brush the dough of each calzone skin with a little olive oil. Divide the roasted peppers among the 4 calzones, placing them on half of the skin and leaving about a 3/4-inch margin. Next, divide the cheese among the 4 servings, placing it on top of the peppers. Fold the dough over and seal the edges tightly, either by pinching them with your fingers or by pressing them together with the tines of a fork. Brush the top of each calzone with a little olive oil and set them on a baking sheet that has been sprinkled with polenta or on pizza stones. Bake in a 500°F oven until the crust turns golden, about 20 minutes. Serve immediately, with the tomato concassé on the side.

Note: To roast peppers, blacken their skins over hot coals, over a flame, or under a broiler, and then place them in a paper or plastic bag for 20 minutes. Remove them from the bag, cut out the cores, pull out the seeds and inner fibers, and rub off the blackened skin.

# Tomato Pasta

Serves 3 or 4 as a main course, or 6 as a first course

You do not need a pasta machine to make homemade pasta, but if you have one, by all means use it. The instructions here are for those who don't have such an appliance. Although this fresh pasta can be cut into any shape—ravioli, lasagne, tortellini, and so on—I prefer it as fettuccine, which I like to dress with a simple dried-tomato cream sauce (page 247).

1²/₃ cups all-purpose flour	2 tablespoons dried-tomato
2 whole eggs	purée or Dried-Tomato
	Pesto (page 246)

Place the flour, 1 egg, and the tomato purée or pesto in a food processor and pulse until the mixture is well combined. Add the second egg and pulse again until the dough is uniformly moist and crumbly. Turn the dough out onto a floured work surface, gather it together, and knead it for 7 to 10 minutes, until it is smooth. Let it rest, covered with a towel or bowl, for 45 minutes.

To begin rolling out the dough, which will be very stiff, flatten it by pressing it very firmly with a rolling pin until it forms a circle. (If your work surface is particularly small, cut the dough in half and roll it out in 2 batches; it becomes quite large as it stretches.) Then press firmly and evenly until the dough is paper thin, about 5 to 10 minutes depending on your strength. Hang the strip of pasta dough on a drying rack over the edge of your cutting board or over a broom handle and let it air-dry for about 10 minutes. Return the sheet of dough to your work surface and sprinkle it lightly with flour. To make fettuccine, roll up the dough lengthwise and, using a very sharp knife, cut through the roll at intervals slightly less than $1/4$ inch. At this point, you will have pasta pinwheels that you must unravel carefully. Sprinkle the dough with a bit of flour or fine cornmeal and let it rest, covered with a towel, for up to an hour.

Cook the fettuccine in a large pot of boiling, salted water for $1^{1}/_{2}$ or 2 minutes, until there is still a bit of resistance at the center of the pasta. Drain it, rinse it in warm water, and drain it again thoroughly. Toss the pasta with butter and fresh basil or other sauce and serve immediately.

VARIATION:

TOMATO-PEPPER PASTA: Use 2 tablespoons double-concentrated tomato paste, 2 teaspoons finely ground black peppercorns, and 1 teaspoon kosher salt in place of the dried-tomato purée.

❦ *Eggs Poached in Tomato Sauce*

Serves 4

Eggs served, and often cooked, in tomato sauce are a traditional dish in several cultures. In the United States, we probably know it best as the Italian Uova in Purgatorio *or the Mexican* Huevos Rancheros. *The combination is infamously delicious, and one variation or another is frequently found on brunch menus in both ethnic and American restaurants. This version, which uses vinegar to accent the tomato's flavor, is wonderful served atop thick slices of grilled or toasted country-style bread. It is also delightful served over grilled polenta.*

2 tablespoons pure olive oil

1 small red onion, peeled and diced

1 cup chicken stock

2 cups tomato sauce, fresh, home-canned, or commercial

Pinch of granulated sugar

1/4 teaspoon crushed red pepper

1 tablespoon red wine vinegar, medium acid

Kosher salt and freshly ground black pepper

4 large eggs

4 thick slices of country-style bread

2 cloves of garlic, cut in half

2 teaspoons minced fresh Italian parsley

Heat the olive oil in a large, heavy frypan and sauté the onion until it is fragrant and tender, about 10 minutes. Add the chicken stock and reduce over medium heat by one-half. Stir in the tomatoes, lower the heat, and simmer for 30 minutes. Taste the sauce, and if it is particularly acidic, add a pinch of granulated sugar. Stir in the crushed red pepper and the vinegar and season to taste with salt and several turns of pepper. The sauce can be made a day or two in advance. Bring it to a simmer in a large, wide pan to complete the dish.

With the sauce hot in a large, low, heavy pan, gently break the eggs, one by one, onto a saucer and then slide them into the sauce, spacing them around the outer edge so as not to crowd them. When all 4 eggs have been added, spoon a little sauce over the top of each, cover the pan, and simmer briefly, until the eggs are just set but the yolks still liquid.

While the eggs cook, quickly toast, broil, or grill the bread, rub each slice with a cut clove of garlic, and place a slice apiece on 4 plates. Using a large, slotted spoon, transfer an egg to each slice. Divide the remaining sauce among the 4 servings and top each with a sprinkling of parsley and a couple of turns of black pepper. Serve immediately.

🧅 Pasta with Uncooked Summer Tomato Sauce with Eight Variations

Serves 3 to 4

One of the simple pleasures of summer is the speed with which bright, elegant meals can be put together. After you have been sated by the first of the tomato harvest, you can get on with doing a little more with summer's finest fruit than plucking it off the vine and eating it. There are endlesss variations to uncooked tomato sauces, and I offer here the basic formula for pasta for 4, along with numerous variations. For the simplest and most casual of sauces, do not peel or seed the tomatoes.

2 pounds medium to large ripe tomatoes (3 to 6 tomatoes, depending on size)

2 whole cloves of garlic, peeled

1 small bunch fresh basil

$^1/_2$ cup extra-virgin olive oil

Kosher salt and freshly ground black pepper

12 ounces pasta (vermicelli, spaghettini, spaghetti)

Discard the stem end of the tomatoes. With a sharp knife, chop the tomatoes coarsely and place them in a glass or stainless-steel bowl. Crush each garlic clove by setting it on your work surface and using your fist to firmly press the side of a knife blade down on it. After smashing the garlic, chop it finely and add it to the tomatoes. Remove the basil leaves from their stems, chop the leaves coarsely, and toss them with the tomatoes and garlic. Add the olive oil and toss again. Let the mixture rest in a cool spot, but not the refrigerator, for about 2 hours.

Cook the pasta and drain it. Season the tomato sauce with salt and pepper and add the pasta to the sauce. Toss the mixture and serve immediately.

VARIATIONS:

MINT: Use $^1/_2$ cup julienned mint leaves instead of the basil.

FETA CHEESE: Add $^3/_4$ cup feta cheese, cut into $^1/_4$-inch cubes, to the sauce.

SPICY: Add 1 serrano or jalapeño pepper, seeded and minced, with the garlic, and use $^1/_2$ cup cilantro leaves in place of the basil.

RED ONION: Add 1 small red onion, diced, to the sauce.

ANCHOVY: Mince 3 small anchovy fillets and add them, with 1 tablespoon red wine vinegar, to the sauce.

PERNOD: Dice 1 medium fennel bulb and add it to the sauce, along with 1 to 2 tablespoons of Pernod.

HONEY-PEPPER: Add 2 tablespoons of honey mixed with 2 tablespoons balsamic vinegar to the tomato mixture. After tossing the pasta with the sauce, add plenty of freshly ground black pepper and toss again.

OLIVES: Reduce the amount of tomatoes to $1^1/_2$ pounds. Add $^1/_2$ cup each sliced pitted green olives and sliced pitted Kalamata olives. Instead of the bunch of basil, use 2 tablespoons chopped fresh oregano, 2 tablespoons chopped fresh basil, and 1 teaspoon fresh thyme leaves.

LASAGNE: Instead of thin strands of pasta, use lasagne. Immediately after cooking them, drain and rinse them and toss with just enough olive oil to coat them. This will discourage their sticking to each other, as lasagne will sometimes do.

✿ Spaghettini with Kalamata Olives & Tomato Concassé

Serves 3 to 4

I find this combination of flavors bright and refreshing in the dead of summer when we are all wilting from the heat. In addition, the sauce requires no cooking, so time at the stove is limited to getting the pasta in and out of the water.

12 ounces dried spaghettini
1 cup Kalamata olives, pitted
6 cloves garlic, peeled
About 16 medium basil leaves

Black pepper in a mill
$3/4$ cup Tomato Concassé (page 231)
$1/2$ cup extra-virgin olive oil
Kosher salt

Cook the pasta in plenty of boiling salted water. While the pasta cooks, place the olives, garlic, and half of the basil leaves in a food processor fitted with its metal blade. Pulse the mixture until the garlic is finely chopped and the olives, garlic, and basil are well blended. Transfer the mixture to a large nonreactive serving bowl, add a few turns of black pepper, and fold in $1/2$ cup of the concassé. Stir in the olive oil, taste, and add a pinch of salt if necessary. When the pasta is just done—but still has a bit of bite at its center—transfer it to a colander or strainer and drain it well, but do not rinse it. Add the pasta to the bowl with the sauce and toss gently until the pasta is thoroughly coated. Either serve in the bowl or divide among 4 warmed plates. Top the pasta with the remaining concassé. Quickly cut the remaining basil leaves into thin julienne (called a chiffonade) and scatter a bit over the pasta. Serve immediately.

VARIATION:

DIJON MUSTARD: Do not add the tomato concassé to the chopped olives. Instead, stir in 2 teaspoons good Dijon mustard and continue the recipe as directed. Add an additional teaspoon of mustard to the concassé and top each serving with a generous spoonful.

🕸 Linguine with Tomatoes, Oranges, Fennel, Currants, & Olives

If you like the slightly bitter taste of oil-cured or salt-cured olives, use them in this sweet and tart pasta. For a milder effect, use Kalamata olives, or even California black olives.

1/4 cup currants
1/2 cup orange juice
4 ripe tomatoes, peeled, seeded, and diced
2 cloves garlic, minced
1 teaspoon minced ginger
1 fennel bulb, trimmed and cut into small dice
2 tablespoons snipped chives
2/3 cup olives, pitted (oil-cured, salt-cured, or Kalamata)

1 orange, peeled, cut into sections with membrane removed
1/2 cup extra-virgin olive oil
2 teaspoons freshly cracked black pepper
Kosher salt
8 to 12 ounces dried linguine
Several leaves of radicchio
1/2 cup pine nuts, toasted

Place the currants in a small bowl and pour the orange juice over them. Let rest for 30 minutes. Toss together the tomatoes, garlic, ginger, fennel, chives, and olives. Cut the sections of orange in half and add them to the vegetables. Add the olive oil and pepper and toss together lightly. When they are finished soaking, add the currants with the orange juice, toss again, and season with a heavy pinch of salt. Let the sauce sit for 1 hour at room temperature before serving.

Cook the linguine in plenty of boiling, salted water until just done. Drain it and rinse it under cool water. Toss the pasta with a very small amount of olive oil and set it aside until ready to serve.

To serve, place 1 or 2 radicchio leaves on individual serving plates, reserving 2 or 3 leaves for garnish. Toss the pasta with half of the sauce and half of the pine nuts and divide it among the servings. Spoon the remaining sauce over the pasta. Quickly cut the remaining radicchio into very thin julienne and garnish each serving with it and the rest of the pine nuts.

🧅 Linguine with Chèvre, Fresh Herbs, & Sautéed Tomatoes

Serves 3 to 4

This simple pasta is quick to make and offers a hearty but not heavy meal, ideal when a summer's night turns cool.

12 ounces dried linguine
3 to 6 tablespoons extra-virgin olive oil
3 cloves garlic, peeled
3 cups cherry tomatoes, cut in half, or 4 medium slicing tomatoes, cut in wedges
¹/₂ cup homemade chicken stock

4 ounces young chèvre, such as chabis or Montrechet
¹/₂ cup fresh minced herbs (basil, thyme, oregano, marjoram, Italian parsley, summer savory, chives)
Kosher salt and freshly ground black pepper

Cook the linguine in plenty of boiling, salted water until just done. While it cooks, warm about 2 tablespoons of olive oil in a heavy skillet, add the garlic, and sauté until it just begins to color. Remove and discard the garlic. Sauté the tomatoes quickly, agitating the pan so that they cook evenly. If using slicing tomatoes, turn the wedges once. Transfer the tomatoes to a warm serving bowl. Add the chicken stock to the skillet, swirl to pick up any pan juices, and reduce by one-third.

Drain the pasta and add it to the bowl on top of the tomatoes. Crumble the goat cheese over the pasta, add the herbs, and pour the chicken stock over all. Add 2 tablespoons of olive oil, toss quickly and lightly with 2 forks, season with salt and pepper, and serve immediately, with the remaining olive oil on the side for those who want it.

🧅 Linguine with Bacon, Goat Cheese, & Sun-dried Tomatoes

Serves 2 to 3

This is a good, quick sauce to use in the late winter, when tomatoes are out of season but there's a fresh crop of arugula, which prefers cooler temperatures.

$^1/_4$ pound bacon or pancetta

4 cloves garlic, slivered

1 bunch arugula, rinsed, trimmed, and cut in strips

$^1/_4$ cup minced sun-dried tomatoes (dry)

8 ounces fresh linguine or tagliarini

5 ounces chèvre (chabis), crumbled

Kosher salt and freshly ground black pepper

6 dried-tomato halves, packed in oil, cut in lengthwise strips

Sauté the bacon until it is just crisp and then transfer it to absorbent paper. Let the bacon drippings cool slightly.

Sauté the garlic in the drippings until it is lightly browned. Add the arugula, toss quickly, and cover the pan, letting the arugula wilt. Remove the lid, add the sun-dried tomatoes, stir, and set the sauce aside. Chop or crumble the bacon and set it aside.

Cook the pasta in rapidly boiling, salted water until it is *just* done. Drain the pasta, transfer it to a large, warmed serving bowl, and top with the arugula mixture. Toss quickly, add the crumbled chèvre, salt and pepper, and toss again. Top with the strips of sun-dried tomatoes and crumbled bacon and serve immediately.

✿ Tomato Pasta with Chicken, Olives, & Dried-Tomato Cream Sauce

Serves 3 to 4

Dried-tomato cream sauce adds a richness to this simple yet hearty pasta dish, perfect as a quick dinner when there's some leftover chicken in the refrigerator.

Dried-Tomato Cream Sauce (page 247)

1 recipe Tomato Pasta (page 150) or 12 ounces imported dried fettuccine

$^1/_2$ cup pitted olives, sliced
  (Kalamata, Niçoise, or
  California black ripe)
12 ounces cooked chicken
  meat (preferably, dark

meat), cut in strips,
  warmed
4 small sprigs fresh thyme
8 marinated dried-tomato
  halves, 4 cut in julienne

Prepare the sauce and make the pasta in advance. Warm the sauce. Cook the pasta in plenty of salted, boiling water. Drain it, add it immediately to the warmed sauce, and toss well to coat. Add the olives and chicken, toss again, and transfer the pasta to a serving platter or 4 warmed plates. Garnish with the sprigs of thyme and the dried tomatoes.

🕷 *Venera's* Gudene

Serves 6 to 8

This recipe came to me from my Sicilian friend A.J., who remembers his mother making it on Sundays. When we decided to revive her old recipe, it took us quite a while to locate the pork skin. We waited for a phone call from the butcher, which finally came one Friday afternoon. "We have some pork skin for you," we were told, and by Saturday we had assembled all the ingredients and spent a wonderful winter's day cooking. It was well worth the wait; the succulent pork-skin rolls contribute a luscious richness to the tomato sauce.

I have encountered just a couple of people who know this dish, friends whose parents come from Italy and who remember it as part of their childhood fare. The name itself is likely derived from cotenna, Italian for pork skin. I've found nothing written on this hearty production, but it seems apparent from the ingredients that this is the sort of cooking that arose from the family farm where all parts of the animal were used, including, as we see here, the skin. Because we have come so very far from living in this way, this is the sort of meal that will not likely be repeated often in our modern home kitchens. And no, this dish does not pay attention to today's compelling health issues. Rather, it is a delicious gesture to a former time and a style of living that is as appealing as it is rare today. And what great fun. Be sure to have some hearty red wine to refresh you during your preparation.

PORK-SKIN ROLLS:

2 or 3 sheets of pork skin
Salt and pepper
1 head garlic, cloves separated, peeled, and minced

1 bunch Italian parsley, minced
1 tablespoon lemon zest, finely minced
$3/4$ cup pine nuts
Olive oil

SAUCE:

1 yellow onion, chopped
5 whole cloves of garlic
3 large cans crushed tomatoes

2 cans tomato purée (not paste)
2 teaspoons dried basil
4 teaspoons dried oregano
Salt and pepper

MEAT BALLS AND SAUSAGES:

$3/4$ pound ground beef
$1/2$ pound ground pork
$1/2$ cup, approximately, bread crumbs (should equal about $1/4$ the volume of the meat mixture)

$1/2$ cup, approximately, grated dried pecorino (again, should equal about $1/4$ the volume of the meat mixture)
1 bunch Italian parsley, minced

2 cloves garlic, minced
Salt and pepper
4 eggs
1 pound (6 to 8) Italian
   sausages

2 pounds dried spaghetti
Olive oil (optional)
2 tablespoons red pepper
   flakes

Trim off excess fat from the pork skins so that there is a scant $1/4$-inch layer of fat remaining. Cut them into rectangles of approximately 6 by 8 inches and place them fat side down on your work surface. Cover the skin side with plenty of salt, pepper, minced garlic, parsley, lemon zest, and pine nuts, dividing the ingredients evenly between the 2 or 3 pieces of skin. Roll up tightly and tie securely with string. The fat will be on the outside.

Add a small amount of olive oil to a large, heavy pot and lightly brown the rolls over a low flame. Remove them from the pan, set them aside, and prepare the sauce.

Using the pan drippings, sauté the onions and garlic until the onions are soft and fragrant, about 15 minutes. When the garlic is just lightly browned, remove it from the pot and discard. Add the remaining sauce ingredients, stir well, and simmer over extremely low heat for $2\frac{1}{2}$ to 3 hours. When the sauce has been simmering about 1 hour, add the pork-skin rolls and continue to cook.

While the sauce is cooking, make the meatballs. Mix together the beef, pork, bread crumbs, cheese, parsley, garlic, salt, pepper, and eggs. Form about 8 flat oblongs that look nothing like standard meatballs, but more like hamburger patties molded for baguettes. Brown the meatballs in a skillet, remove them, and then brown the sausages in the pan drippings. Add the sausages and meatballs to the pot of sauce about 45 minutes before the sauce is done.

Bring a large pot of salted water to a boil and cook the spaghetti *al dente*. Drain it and toss with a little olive oil or a little of the sauce and place on a large serving platter. Spoon plenty of sauce over the pasta and arrange the meatballs and sausages on top. Set the pork-skin rolls on your work surface, cut through the strings, and remove them. Cut the rolls into enough portions to serve all your guests and arrange the rolls on top of the pasta, meatballs, and sausages. Serve immediately, with hot red pepper flakes on the side.

✿ Risotto with Sun-dried Tomatoes, Brie, & Pine Nuts

Serves 6 as a side dish

This creamy risotto is outstanding with simple roasted chicken and Tomatoes Provençal (page 195).

$^1/_4$ cup sun-dried tomato bits	1 small yellow onion, peeled and minced
$^3/_4$ cup dry white wine	1 large shallot, minced
5 cups stock (see Note)	3 cloves garlic, minced
2 tablespoons butter	1 $^1/_2$ cups arborio rice
1 tablespoon pure olive oil	$^1/_2$ cup cream

3 ounces Brie, cut in small
pieces
1/2 cup pine nuts, toasted
3 tablespoons finely minced
fresh Italian parsley or
snipped fresh chives

Kosher salt and freshly
ground black pepper
6 halves sun-dried toma-
toes, packed in oil, cut
in thin strips

Place the sun-dried tomato bits and wine in a nonreactive saucepan, bring to a boil, lower the heat, and simmer until the wine is reduced by one-third. Set aside.

Have stock simmering when you begin the risotto. Melt the butter and olive oil together in a heavy skillet. Add the onion and shallot and sauté until they are tender and fragrant, about 10 minutes, being careful not to brown the vegetables. Add the garlic and sauté for another 2 minutes. Add the rice and cook for 2 minutes, stirring continuously. With the heat at medium, add the hot stock, 1/2 cup at a time, stirring regularly and waiting until the stock is nearly completely absorbed before adding the next portion. When there is just 1 cup of stock remaining, add 1/4 cup at a time. When done, in about 15 to 20 minutes, the rice will be tender but retain its separate shape and have a bit of resistance at its center.

After the final addition of stock, stir in the sun-dried tomatoes and wine, the cream, and the cheese and remove the risotto from the heat immediately. Stir in the pine nuts and half of the parsley or chives. Taste the risotto and season with salt and pepper. Divide among warmed serving plates and garnish each portion with strips of sun-dried tomato and a sprinkling of the remaining parsley or chives. Serve immediately.

🧅 *Fresh Tomato Pie*

It seems everyone has a variation of this tomato pie, and well they should; it's great. Laurie Colwin, in More Home Cooking, *gives a narrative version similar to the one here that uses canned tomatoes, making it an easy year-round recipe. Lee Bailey's charming little book* Tomatoes *offers a great version. And in* Gourmet *magazine in some long-lost issue was a recipe passed on to me by a friend of a friend, who made it all summer long, he told me. Here I add my version to the lot, along with a sassy heated-up version.*

2 cups all-purpose flour
2 teaspoons black pepper-
   corns, crushed fine
Kosher salt
1 tablespoon baking pow-
   der
1 stick ($^{1}/_{4}$ pound) butter,
   chilled and cut into $^{1}/_{4}$-
   inch cubes
$^{2}/_{3}$ cup whole milk
$2^{1}/_{2}$ to 3 pounds medium-
   sized ripe slicing tomatoes, peeled, seeded,
   and thickly sliced

Large bunch fresh basil
4 ounces (2 cups) grated
   medium-sharp or sharp
   cheddar cheese
$^{2}/_{3}$ cup homemade or best-
   quality mayonnaise
$^{1}/_{2}$ lemon
2 or 3 tablespoons heavy
   cream

Sift or mix together the flour, the pepper, 1 teaspoon salt, and the baking powder. Either by hand using a pastry blender or in a food processor, quickly work the butter into the flour mixture so that it has the consistency of coarse-grain sand. If using a food processor, add the milk, pulse quickly quickly 2 or 3 times—until the dough just barely comes together—and then turn it out onto a floured surface. If working by hand, make a small well in the center of the flour, pour the milk in, and then mix quickly with a fork until the dough comes together but is still soft and sticky. Turn onto a floured surface.

Knead the dough for about 30 seconds and then let it rest for 10 minutes. Cut the dough in half, roll out one half to fit a 10-inch pie pan, and line the pan with it.

Cover the surface of the pie with a layer of tomatoes, sprinkle with a little salt, and add a sparse layer of basil leaves; repeat for a second, third, and fourth layer. Top with the grated cheese. Thin the mayonnaise with the juice of $1/2$ lemon and spread it over the surface. Quickly roll out the reserved dough, fit it over the pie, and seal the edges by pinching them together. Cut several slits in the dough to allow steam to escape and brush the surface with the heavy cream. Bake in a 350°F oven until the pie is hot all the way through and the crust is golden, about 25 to 30 minutes. Let rest for 15 minutes before serving. Cut it in wedges and garnish each slice with a sprig of basil.

VARIATION:
SPICY: Substitute cilantro for the basil, Monterey Jack cheese for the cheddar, and Chipotle Mayonnaise (page 255) thinned with lime juice in place of the basic mayonnaise.

Tomato & Polenta Tart with Basil Mayonnaise

Serves 4 to 6

I could eat this tart every day during tomato season. It is wonderful straight from the oven with freshly picked salad greens on the side, and equally delicious the next day, cold, right out of the refrigerator. It also reheats quite well.

2¹/₂ cups water
¹/₂ cup polenta
2 tablespoons butter
2 teaspoons kosher salt
¹/₄ cup all-purpose flour
1 cup basil leaves, loosely packed
4 medium-sized ripe slicing tomatoes

Salt and freshly ground black pepper
4 ounces cheese (cheddar, jack, or other mild-to-medium sharp semisoft cheese), grated
Juice of ¹/₂ lemon
³/₄ cup homemade or best-quality mayonnaise

Place the water in a heavy saucepan and stir in the polenta. Set over medium heat and bring to a boil, stirring constantly. Reduce the heat and simmer the polenta for about 10 minutes, stirring constantly until it thickens and then stirring frequently. Add the butter and stir the polenta until the butter is melted. Add the kosher salt and flour and stir continuously until the mixture is thick and pulls away from the side of the pan, about 4 to 5 minutes. Remove from the heat and pour into a 10- or 12-inch tart pan that has been coated with a bit of olive oil. Using a rubber spatula, press the polenta to the bottom and sides of the pan so that it forms a sort of crust. The polenta will be softer than chilled pie dough, but it will hold its shape. Set the shell aside until it firms up, about 20 minutes.

Peel the tomatoes, cut off the stem ends, and slice them in $1/4$-inch rounds. Cover the surface of the polenta shell with some of the basil leaves and arrange the tomatoes on top, making two layers and topping each layer with a bit of salt and pepper and half of the cheese. Bake in a 325°F oven for about 20 minutes, until the tart is hot and slightly bubbly and the top is just turning golden.

Meanwhile, place the remaining basil leaves and the lemon juice in a blender and pulse until the basil is puréed. Add the mayonnaise, pulse the mixture very quickly to blend well, transfer it to a serving bowl, taste, and season with salt and pepper.

Remove the tart from the oven, let rest for 15 minutes, drizzle basil mayonnaise over the surface, cut the tart into wedges, and serve it, with more basil mayonnaise on the side.

 *Ratatouille*

This ratatouille combines two techniques to create a rich and evocative version of the famous vegetable stew from the south of France. Some of the vegetables are roasted together, so that their flavors mingle from the start; others are cooked separately so that they retain their unique flavor and don't overpower the other ingredients. When all are cooked properly, they are mixed together and allowed to rest for an hour, their juices mingling and enriching one another but not to an overwhelming degree. I find this method produces the best ratatouille I've had. It is excellent with grilled sausages as an accompaniment.

8 ounces peeled cloves of garlic

8 ounces crimini or standard white mushrooms, small and whole

2 eggplants, peeled and cut into 1-inch cubes

3 medium or 4 small yellow onions, peeled and cut into quarters

1 3/4 cups pure olive oil

2 sprigs fresh thyme

1 sprig fresh oregano

2 pounds ripe red tomatoes

3 sweet red peppers, stemmed, cored, and cut into medium julienne

4 zucchini, cut into medium julienne

1/4 cup finely minced fresh Italian parsley

2 tablespoons finely minced fresh basil

Kosher salt and freshly ground black pepper

Toss the whole cloves of garlic, mushrooms, eggplant, and onions together and place them in a heavy roasting pan. Pour 1 1/4 cups of the olive oil over them, add the sprigs of thyme and oregano, and cover the pan with aluminum foil. Bake at 350°F for 1 hour.

While the vegetables roast, peel the tomatoes by holding each one over a flame and quickly blistering its skin, letting it cool, and removing the charred skin. Cut the tomatoes in half and gently squeeze out seeds and excess moisture. In another roasting pan, add a little olive oil and then set the tomatoes in a flat layer, cut side down. Roast in the oven with the other vegetables until the tomatoes begin to darken and caramelize, 40 to 60 minutes.

Heat a small amount of the remaining olive oil in a heavy skillet and sauté the sweet peppers until they are limp and fragrant. Transfer them to another container and sauté the zucchini until it begins to turn golden brown. Add the zucchini to the peppers.

After 1 hour, test the roasting garlic and other vegetables to be sure they are tender. If not, cover again and let roast an additional 15 minutes. Remove from the oven, discard the sprigs of herbs, and let the vegetables cool slightly. Check the tomatoes and remove them from the oven when they are done. Set a large colander over a bowl, transfer the cooled vegetables to it, and let them sit for about 10 minutes so that any excess olive oil will drain out. Break up the roasted tomatoes with a fork and add them to the peppers and zucchini. Gently toss together all of the vegetables and the minced herbs. Let the vegetables rest together for at least 1 hour so that their flavors can mingle. Taste the ratatouille and season with salt and pepper.

Ratatouille may be served at room temperature, chilled, or heated. To heat, place in a large ovenproof dish and place in a 325°F oven for 20 minutes.

✿ Mexican Seafood Stew with Cilantro Sauce

Serves 4 to 6

The achiote—a paste of ground annato seed, cumin, garlic, vinegar, and oregano—provides the added depth of flavor in this delightful stew, which I have served on many special occasions. Vary the seafood with what is available (and omit the shellfish entirely if you don't feel like being bothered with them), but do make the extra effort to locate the achiote, which can be found in most Mexican and or other Latin markets.

4 tablespoons olive oil

1 cup sliced leeks, white part only

2 or 3 serrano peppers, seeded and diced

6 cloves garlic, minced

4 cups chicken stock

2 tablespoons achiote

1/2 pound new red potatoes or Yellow Finn potatoes, cleaned and diced

2 medium (5-inch) zucchini, diced

2 cups fresh tomato pulp

Kosher salt and freshly ground black pepper

6 ounces small dried pasta (tripolini, farfallini, or small shells)

2 bunches fresh cilantro, cleaned and large stems removed

4 to 6 whole cloves of garlic, peeled

Juice of 1 lime

1/2 cup extra-virgin olive oil

1/2 teaspoon kosher salt

1/2 pound prawns, deveined

1/2 pound fish fillets (snapper is ideal), cut in 1-inch cubes

2 pounds fresh mussels, scrubbed clean, or 2 pounds cherrystone clams

1 whole lime, cut in wedges

Heat the olive oil in a large, heavy pot and sauté the leeks and peppers until they are soft and fragrant, about 15 minutes. Add the garlic and sauté another 2 minutes. Break up the achiote with your fingers and place it in a small bowl. Stir in a little of the stock to thin the paste, and then add the paste and the rest of the stock to the leek mixture. Add the potatoes, let simmer for 10 minutes. Add the zucchini and tomatoes, and simmer the mixture for another 5 minutes. Taste and season as needed with salt and pepper.

While the vegetables are cooking, cook the pasta separately and make the cilantro sauce. Place the cilantro, garlic, and lime juice in a blender and pulse until puréed. Add the olive oil and $1/2$ teaspoon kosher salt and pulse until smooth. Transfer the cilantro sauce to a small serving bowl. Drain and rinse the pasta, toss it with 2 tablespoons of the cilantro sauce, and set it aside.

Add the seafood to the vegetables, cover the pot, cook for just 5 minutes, and remove from the heat. Divide the pasta among heated soup bowls and then ladle the stew over it, being sure that each serving receives some of each type of seafood. Top each portion with a spoonful of cilantro sauce and serve immediately, with a wedge of lime on the side.

❦ Mussels with Tomatoes, Garlic, Chorizo, & White Wine

Serves 4

I like this dish in the fall, with the last of the season's tomatoes and plump, juicy mussels from the coast near my Northern California home.

1 pound chorizo sausage
1 serrano pepper, minced
3 pounds fresh mussels in their shells
2 tablespoons pure olive oil
Handful garlic cloves
2 shallots
2 cups dry white wine
Juice of 1 or 2 lemons ($^1/_4$ cup juice)
1 bay leaf
2 cups fresh tomato pulp

$^1/_2$ teaspoon crushed red pepper
2 tablespooons minced fresh Italian parsley
3 tablespoons minced fresh cilantro
Kosher salt and freshly ground pepper
2 tablespoons extra-virgin olive oil
Aioli (page 254) or cilantro sauce (page 97)

Fry the chorizo with the serrano pepper, crumbling the meat with a fork, until it is just done. Drain off excess fat and set the mixture aside. Scrub the mussels, cut the beards, and rinse in plenty of fresh, clean water. Heat the olive oil in a large, heavy pot, and sauté the shallots and garlic for 3 minutes. Add the white wine, lemon juice, bay leaf, and mussels, bring the wine to a simmer, cover the pot, and cook until the mussels just begin to open, 4 to 5 minutes. Using a slotted spoon, transfer the mussels to a large serving bowl and keep them warm.

Strain the broth into another pot and add the tomatoes and crushed red pepper. Bring to a simmer, cook 3 or 4 minutes, and remove from the heat. Stir in the parsley, the cilantro, and the chorizo and serrano mixture, and taste the broth. Season with salt and pepper to taste, add the olive oil, but do not stir again. Pour the broth over the mussels and serve immediately, with Aioli (page 254) or cilantro sauce on the side.

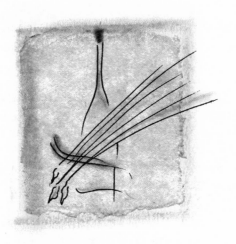

✿ Scallops with Roasted-Tomato Sauce, Preserved Garlic, & Aioli

Serves 3 to 4

The flavors in this simple dish are sensational, and it is perfect as a light main course during hot weather. Be sure to serve with a good, crusty bread.

12 large sea scallops	Simple Roasted-Tomato
Olive oil or duck fat	Sauce (page 238)
Kosher salt and freshly	Preserved garlic (see Note)
ground black pepper	Aioli (optional, page 254)

Sauté scallops in olive oil or duck fat until just done, about 3 minutes on each side. Season with salt and pepper, remove from heat, and keep warm.

In the center of each of 4 serving plates, spoon about $1/2$ cup roasted-tomato sauce, and set 3 scallops on the edge of the sauce. Spoon several cloves of preserved garlic over the dish, top each scallop with a small spoonful of aioli, and serve immediately.

Note: To make preserved garlic, place 1 cup whole garlic cloves, peeled, in a small saucepan and cover them with extra-virgin olive oil. Set over a medium flame, bring to a simmer, and lower the heat so that the garlic *barely* simmers in the oil for 30 minutes. Remove from the heat and let cool. Use immediately or store garlic and oil in a covered jar in the refrigerator.

Red Snapper with Kalamata Risotto, Golden Tomato Coulis, & Warm Tomato-Olive Vinaigrette

Serves 4

Made at the peak of tomato season, this risotto, a glorious combination of both colors and flavors, is the very essence of summer. Although its preparation is not at all complicated, it does take a bit of time because of the two sauces, making it ideal for a special occasion when the extra effort is warranted.

4 fillets of red snapper, approximately 6 ounces each

Kosher salt and freshly ground black pepper

5 cups stock (see Note, page 104)

2 tablespoons butter

1 tablespoon pure olive oil

1 small yellow onion, peeled and minced

1 1/2 cups arborio rice

1/2 cup (about 1 ounce) cheese, grated (Dry Jack, Romano, Parmigiano, aged Asiago)

1/2 cup finely minced Kalamata olives

Golden Tomato Coulis (page 232)

Warm Tomato-Olive Vinaigrette (page 252)

Italian parsley sprigs

Several whole Kalamata olives for garnish

Prepare the snapper for broiling so that it can be ready at the same time as the risotto. Have the broiler preheated and the fish on a rack, seasoned with salt and pepper. When the risotto is about half done, place the snapper under the broiler about 4 inches from the heat and cook without turning until the flesh is entirely white, about 7 to 9 minutes.

Have stock simmering when you begin the risotto. Melt the butter and olive oil together in a heavy skillet. Add the onion and sauté until it is tender and fragrant, about 10 minutes, being careful not to brown it. Add the rice, stir into the onion, and cook for 2 minutes. With the heat at medium, add the hot stock, $1/2$ cup at a time, stirring regularly and waiting until the stock is nearly completely absorbed before adding the next portion. When there is just 1 cup of stock remaining, add $1/4$ cup at a time. When the rice is done, after about 15 to 20 minutes, it will be tender but retain its separate shape and have a bit of resistance at its center. After the final addition of stock, remove the risotto from the heat immediately and stir in the cheese and minced olives. Taste the risotto and season with salt and pepper as needed.

Remove the snapper from the oven. Spoon about $1/2$ cup of the coulis onto 4 serving plates and agitate the plates so that the sauce spreads evenly over the surface. Place risotto in the center of each plate and set a fillet of snapper, half on the risotto and half on the sauce, on each plate. Spoon about $1/4$ cup of the warm vinaigrette down the center of the snapper. Garnish each serving with a sprig of Italian parsley and several whole olives. Serve immediately.

❧ Risotto with Fillet of Salmon and Tomato Concassé

Serves 4

The bright, fresh flavor of the tomatoes makes this a perfect meal on a summer evening. Serve it with zucchini sautéed quickly in butter and seasoned with plenty of freshly ground black pepper.

4 fillets of salmon, about
  6 ounces each
Kosher salt and freshly
  ground black pepper
4 cups stock
1 cup dry white wine
2 tablespoons butter
1 tablespoon pure olive oil

1 small yellow onion,
  peeled and minced
1 ½ cups arborio rice
2 cups Tomato Concassé
  (page 231)
1 cup grated cheese (Dry
  Jack or aged Asiago)
2 tablespoons snipped
  chives

Arrange the fish fillets on a heavy baking sheet and season them with salt and pepper. Place the fish in a preheated, 400°F oven about 8 to 10 minutes before the risotto has finished cooking.

  Combine the stock and the wine and bring it to a steady simmer before you begin the risotto. Melt the butter and olive oil together in a heavy skillet. Add the onion and sauté until it is tender and fragrant, about 10 minutes, being careful not to brown it. Add the rice, stir into the onion, and cook for 2 minutes. With the heat at medium, add the hot stock, $^1/_2$ cup at a time, stirring regularly and waiting until the stock is nearly completely absorbed before adding the next portion. When just 1 cup of stock remains, add $^1/_4$ cup at a time. When done, in about 15 to 20 minutes, the rice will be tender but retain its separate shape and have a bit of resistance at its center. After the final addition of stock, stir in 1 cup of the concassé, remove the risotto from the heat, and stir in the cheese. Taste the risotto and season with salt and pepper.

Remove the salmon from the oven. Divide the risotto among 4 warmed serving plates and top each serving with a fillet. Divide the remaining concassé between the servings, placing it on top of the salmon. Garnish with the snipped chives and serve immediately.

❧ Lamb Patties with White Beans & Tomato-Mustard Coulis

Serves 6

Here, a tomato coulis spiked with mustard ties together creamy white beans and savory, mustard-scented lamb. Heavenly.

1 $^1/_2$ cups dry white beans, soaked in water over-night and drained

3 cups lamb or duck stock
3 cups water

Kosher salt and freshly
  ground black pepper
2 tablespoons olive oil
2 shallots, minced
4 to 6 cloves garlic,
  peeled and minced
2 teaspoons white mustard
  seeds, soaked in enough
  water to cover
1 1/2 pounds lean ground
  lamb

1 teaspoon, plus 1 table-
  spoon Dijon mustard
2 tablespoons fresh herbs
  (a mix of snipped
  chives, Italian parsley,
  cilantro, and oregano)
Red or Golden Tomato
  Coulis (pages 233 or
  232)
1 tablespoon coarse-grain
  mustard (not sweet)

In a heavy pot, combine the beans, stock, and water and
simmer until the beans are very tender but not falling apart,
about 30 minutes. Remove from the heat, let the beans cool
in the stock, and then drain them. Season with salt and
pepper.

While the beans cook, heat the olive oil in a small,
heavy skillet, and sauté the shallots and garlic until they are
soft. Drain the mustard seeds and add them to the shallots.
In a mixing bowl, combine the lamb with the sautéed shallot mixture, 1 teaspoon of Dijon mustard, and the fresh
herbs. Season with salt and pepper. Form into 6 patties
about 3/4 inch thick.

Heat the tomato coulis, stir in the tablespoon of Dijon
mustard, and the coarse-grain mustard and taste the sauce.
Adjust the seasoning, adding more Dijon, salt, or pepper for
a well-balanced sauce.

Grill, fry, or broil the lamb patties until they are medium rare, about 6 or 7 minutes on the first side, about 5
minutes after turning. Remove from the heat.

To serve, ladle some of the tomato coulis onto each of 6 warmed serving plates. Set a lamb patty off center on each plate and spoon a mound of beans next to it. Drizzle a bit more sauce over the lamb and sprinkle pepper over each serving. Serve immediately.

🧄 Oven-roasted Lamb with Onions, Potatoes, Tomatoes, & Rosemary

Serves 6 to 8

I have come across several versions of this traditional Provençal method of preparing lamb. Because I love garlic and particularly its flavor when roasted in the juices of the lamb, I have included garlic cloves in my version of the traditional recipe.

1 full leg of lamb, trimmed of the fell and extra fat
3 cloves garlic, sliced, plus 20 cloves, peeled
2 to 3 tablespoons extra-virgin olive oil
1 pound Red Bliss potatoes, cut in $1/4$-inch rounds

2 yellow onions, sliced
6 to 8 large red tomatoes, stem end removed, cut in $1/4$-inch slices
Rosemary sprigs, for cooking and for garnish
Salt and freshly ground pepper

After trimming the lamb, make numerous slits in the flesh with the tip of a knife and tuck a slice of garlic into each cut. Set the lamb on a roasting rack and heat the oven to 325°F. Brush the inside of a roasting pan that is at least 2$^1/_2$ inches deep with a generous coating of olive oil. Spread the potatoes over the surface of the pan, overlapping them slightly if necessary. Top the potatoes with the onion slices and scatter the whole garlic cloves over the onions. Place the tomato slices on top, overlapping them slightly so that they all fit in a single layer. Tuck in the sprigs of rosemary here and there between the tomato slices.

Set the rack on top of the pan. The rack should be large enough to suspend the lamb *over* the pan but not down in it, so that the juices of the lamb drip into the vegetables but the lamb doesn't stew with the vegetables. Cook the lamb and vegetables until the lamb is done to your liking. For rare meat, which retains the most flavor, allow about 15 to 16 minutes per pound. Remove the lamb from the oven and let it rest for 15 minutes before carving.

Carve the lamb, place the vegetables on a large platter, and surround them with slices of the meat. If there are any additional pan juices, pour them over the meat and vegetables. Garnish with rosemary sprigs, a sprinkling of salt, and plenty of pepper. Serve immediately.

VARIATION:
Add 1 cup olives of choice to the vegetables along with 1 lemon, thinly sliced and tucked in between slices of tomato.

✿ Lamb Loin & Lemon-scented Risotto with Tomato-Lemon Sauce

Serves 4 to 6

Although we have excellent lamb year round, I love this dish in the spring, when it can be served with tender stalks of asparagus.

2 pounds lamb loin (see Note)
Salt and freshly ground pepper
1 medium sprig rosemary
2 cups duck, veal, or lamb stock diluted with water to make 5 cups
1 tablespoon butter
2 tablespoons pure olive oil
1 small yellow onion, peeled and chopped
4 cloves garlic, minced

1 1/2 cups arborio rice
1/4 cup fresh lemon juice
1 tablespoon finely minced lemon zest
1/2 teaspoon finely minced fresh rosemary
1/2 cup grated Romano Pecorino cheese
Tomato-Lemon Sauce (page 245)
1 teaspoon lemon zest in thin strips
4 small sprigs rosemary
4 thin slices lemon

Time the cooking of the lamb so that it is done about 10 minutes before the risotto. To grill the lamb, prepare coals about 45 minutes before cooking time. Salt and pepper the loin and grill, for rare meat, about 7 minutes on each side. To oven roast the loin, brown it quickly in a heavy skillet, place it on a roasting pan, and cook it in a 375°F oven for about 20 minutes. Remove the loin from the oven and let it rest 10 minutes before slicing it crosswise in thin strips.

Add the rosemary sprig to the stock and have it simmering when you begin the risotto. Melt the butter and olive oil together in a heavy skillet. Add the onion and sauté until it is tender and fragrant, about 10 minutes, being careful not to brown it. Add the garlic, sauté 2 minutes, and add the rice. Stirring continuously, cook for 2 minutes. With the heat at medium, add the hot stock, $1/2$ cup at a time, stirring regularly and waiting until the stock is nearly completely absorbed before adding the next portion. When just 1 cup of stock remains, add $1/4$ cup at a time. When done, after about 15 to 20 minutes, the rice will be tender but retain its separate shape and have a bit of resistance at its center. After the final addition of stock, stir in the lemon juice, lemon zest, and minced rosemary, remove the risotto from the heat immediately, and stir in the cheese. Taste the risotto and season with salt and pepper.

Spoon hot tomato-lemon sauce onto warmed serving plates and top with a portion of risotto. Arrange several slices of lamb loin next to the risotto and top with a spoonful of sauce and the strips of lemon zest. Garnish with a small sprig of rosemary and a slice of lemon. Serve immediately.

Note: Ask your butcher for a whole lamb loin, the tender stretch of meat that is more familiar to us as loin chops. If lamb loin is unavailable, substitute about $1^{1}/_{2}$ to 2 pounds of boned leg lamb.

✦ Home-Cured Pork Tenderloin with White Bean Cakes & Tomato-Currant Chutney

Serves 6

Home-cured meats are not as common as they once were in the United States, or as they are today in Europe. Curing meat is really a very easy matter, however; you just need to plan on doing it several days before you need the meat. Here, the actual time spent working on the cured pork is minimal. Certainly, you can make this delightful dish with fresh pork tenderloin, but it won't have the complexity or depth of flavor that cured pork imparts.

2 cured pork tenderloins
  (recipe follows) or 2
  fresh pork tenderloins,
  about 2¹/₂ pounds total
3 tablespoons fresh sage,
  chopped
¹/₂ cup cream
2 tablespoons pure olive
  oil, plus more for
  sautéing
1 small yellow onion, diced
4 to 6 cloves garlic,
  peeled and minced

3 cups cooked white
  beans (cannelini, small,
  or navy)
2 ounces Parmigiano or
  Romano cheese, grated
Kosher salt and freshly
  ground black pepper
¹/₂ cup all-purpose flour
2 to 3 tablespoons butter
Tomato-Currant Chutney
  (page 276)
Small sprigs sage for
  garnish

Set the pork tenderloins on a rack over a sheet pan or roasting pan and place in a 375°F oven for 25 to 35 minutes, until the meat has reached a minimum temperature of at least 145 degrees. Remove it from the oven and let it rest 5 minutes before slicing.

In a small, heavy saucepan combine the sage and cream and bring the mixture to a boil. Reduce the heat, let it simmer until the cream is reduced by half, and then remove it from the heat and let it steep.

Heat the olive oil in a heavy skillet and sauté the onion over medium heat until it is tender and fragrant, about 15 minutes. Add the garlic, sauté another 2 minutes, and then add half the white beans. Stir the mixture and, while it warms, mash the beans with a fork. Strain the sage cream into the mixture and stir quickly to incorporate the cream. Remove from the heat and let it cool slightly. Fold in the whole beans and the cheese, taste the mixture, and season with a pinch of salt and a slightly more generous smount of pepper.

Place the flour in a small, low bowl. Form the bean mixture into rounds about the size of tennis balls and coat each one in flour by placing it into the bowl with the flour and agitating the bowl. Heat the butter in a heavy skillet until it foams. Fry the bean cakes by placing 2 or 3 in the skillet at a time, flattening each with a spatula. Turn the cakes after about 4 minutes and cook until each side is golden.

Set a bean cake on each of 6 warmed serving plates. Slice the tenderloin very thin, and arrange several slices alongside each bean cake. Add a generous spoonful of the chutney to each serving, garnish with a sprig of sage, and serve immediately, with more chutney on the side.

HOME-CURED PORK TENDERLOIN:

2 quarts spring water
8 ounces kosher salt or sea
    salt
8 ounces granulated sugar
2 heaping tablespoons
    saltpeter

1 tablespoon whole black
    peppercorns
2 to 6 pork tenderloins,
    about 16 to 20 ounces
    each

In a heavy stock pot, combine the water, salt, sugar, and saltpeter and bring the liquid to a boil, stirring it occasionally. When the salt and sugar are dissolved, remove the brine from the heat, add the peppercorns, and let the brine cool to room temperature.

Begin the curing process with utensils that are extremely clean and have been rinsed in very hot water. Place the pork tenderloins in a nonreactive container such as plastic, glass, or crockery, and pour the brine over the meat. The pork must be fully submerged in the brine, so choose your container accordingly or increase the amount of brine, proportionately, in order to fully cover the pork. Weight the pork with a plate, a small, clean cutting board, or other suitable object to keep it below the brine. Cover the container and place it either in the refrigerator or, if you are in a particularly cool environment or have a cellar, in a cool, dark place for 6 full days. Remove the pork from the brine and refrigerate it, wrapped or covered, for up to 10 days.

🧅 Beef, Cherry Tomatoes, & Mushrooms on Skewers with Tomato-Garlic Chutney

Serves 6

The ginger in this marinade resonates beautifully with the chutney.

2 pounds beef tenderloin, cut into thin strips
1 cup hearty red wine
$^1/_2$ cup fresh lemon juice
$^1/_2$ cup pure olive oil, plus more as needed
5 cloves garlic, crushed
4 slices fresh ginger
Kosher salt and freshly ground black pepper
3 medium red onions, quartered

Pure olive oil
24 small to medium mushrooms (crimini or shiitake), tough stems removed
1 dozen 12-inch wood skewers, soaked in water for at least 30 minutes
36 cherry tomatoes
Tomato-Garlic Chutney (page 277)

Place the beef in a glass roasting pan or other low, nonreactive container. Mix together the wine, lemon juice, olive oil, garlic, and ginger. Add a teaspoon of salt and some pepper and pour enough of the the marinade over the beef to cover it, reserving the rest. Let the beef rest for at least 1 hour or up to 3 hours before cooking. Refrigerate until 30 minutes before assembly.

Coat the onions in a bit of olive oil and either grill them over medium coals or in a 325°F oven for about 20 minutes, until they have started to get tender. Remove them from the heat, let them cool, and then cut them into quarters. Wash the mushrooms, being sure to remove any pieces of dirt, and pat them dry. Heat several tablespoons of the reserved marinade in a small skillet and cook the mushrooms for 3 to 4 minutes, until they begin to soften. Remove them from the heat and let them cool.

To assemble, thread a strip of beef on each skewer, along with 2 or 3 tomatoes, 2 mushrooms, and a generous piece of onion. Grill over medium coals for just 3 to 4 minutes on each side, until the skins on the tomatoes start to crack and the beef just barely turns color. Transfer the skewers from the grill to a serving platter and serve immediately, with Tomato-Garlic Chutney and any other accompaniments alongside.

❧ Baked Cherry Tomatoes with Three Variations

Serves 4 to 6

I have been making this simple dish for over two decades and I still love it as much as I did the first time I tasted it. It's a wonderful use for excess cherry tomatoes.

1 quart cherry tomatoes, especially Sweet 100s
Handful garlic cloves, peeled and sliced
2 tablespoons snipped chives

$^1/_4$ cup extra-virgin olive oil
Juice of 1 lemon
Black pepper in a mill
Kosher salt

Place the tomatoes in a baking dish, add the garlic and chives, and toss. Pour the olive oil over the tomatoes, followed by the lemon juice. Toss again, season with several turns of black pepper, and place in a 350°F oven for 20 to 30 minutes, until the tomatoes have burst open and the garlic is tender. Remove the tomatoes from the oven and season them with kosher salt to taste. Serve hot, warm, or chilled as a side dish.

VARIATIONS:

PESTO: Before serving, stir in 2 to 3 tablespoons of pesto.

GOAT CHEESE & TAPENADE: Spoon the tomatoes over a log of goat cheese and serve with croutons and a garnish of tapenade. To make a simple tapenade, purée together $1/2$ cup pitted Kalamata olives, 2 or 3 cloves of garlic, peeled, 2 or 3 anchovy fillets, 1 tablespoon Dijon mustard, 1 tablespoon minced fresh Italian parsley, and $1/4$ cup extra-virgin olive oil. Store in the refrigerator for up to 10 days.

ANCHOVY: Add 2 or 3 anchovy fillets to the tomatoes before baking, and use 2 tablespoons of medium-acid red wine vinegar in place of the lemon juice.

☙ Grilled Cherry Tomatoes

Serves 6

Skewers threaded with beautiful ruby-red cherry tomatoes brighten up any outdoor barbecue.

1 dozen 12-inch wooden skewers, soaked in water for 30 minutes	2 small red onions, cut into wedges
4 dozen perfect, ripe cherry tomatoes	Balsamic vinegar Kosher salt and freshly ground black pepper

Thread 4 tomatoes onto each of the 12 skewers, alternating with a single piece of onion. Grill over medium coals, turning every 2 minutes, until the tomatoes begin to crack open and sizzle. Transfer the tomatoes to a serving platter, drizzle with just a bit balsamic vinegar, and season with salt and pepper. Serve immediately.

🍅 Tomatoes Provençal

Serves 6

These classic roasted tomatoes are one of my favorite accompaniments to almost any meal, from roasted chicken to a simple risotto.

6 medium slicing toma-
toes, ripe but slightly
firm
6 cloves garlic, thinly
sliced
4 tablespoons extra-virgin
olive oil

1 teaspoon kosher salt
Black pepper in a mill
1 cup fresh bread crumbs
2 tablespoons finely
minced fresh Italian
parsley

Cut a slice off the stem ends of the tomatoes just above the shoulder (where the tomato begins to widen). Carefully pierce the tomatoes several times with a fork, pointing the tines down directly into the flesh but being careful not to puncture the skin. Place them in a baking dish and top each with several slices of garlic, drizzle with about $1/2$ to 1 teaspoon of olive oil, and season with a pinch of salt and a bit of pepper. Mix together the bread crumbs and parsley and season with a little salt and pepper. Top each tomato with a coating of the bread crumbs and a drizzle of the remaining olive oil.

Bake the tomatoes in a 375°F oven until they are soft and beginning to brown, from 45 to 60 minutes. Remove them from the oven, let them rest 5 minutes, and serve immediately.

❦ *Fried Tomatoes with Herbs & Cream*

Serves 4 to 6

These tomatoes are simply sensational, and the sauce is so full of great flavor that you want to pick up your plate and lick it, so be sure to serve plenty of good bread.

4 large ripe tomatoes
2 tablespoons snipped chives
2 tablespoons minced fresh Italian parsley
2 tablespoons minced fresh cilantro
4 cloves garlic, peeled and minced

2 serrano peppers, peeled and minced
2 tablespoons butter
$1/2$ cup dry white wine
$1/2$ cup heavy cream
Kosher salt and freshly ground black pepper
Fresh herbs (chives, Italian parsley, cilantro), for garnish

Wash the tomatoes, dry them, and cut out their cores. Slice them about $^3/_8$ inch thick and spread them out on a plate or glass baking dish. Sprinkle each of the herbs, the garlic, and the serrano pepper over the tomatoes. Cover the tomatoes with a tea towel and let them rest for about 3 hours.

Heat the butter in a heavy skillet and sauté the tomatoes for about 3 minutes on each side. Sauté in batches so as not to crowd the skillet, and transfer the sautéed tomatoes to a warm serving plate. When all the tomatoes have been cooked, hold them in a warm oven while you complete the sauce.

Pour into the sauté pan any juices that collected while the tomatoes and herbs marinated, along with any herbs, garlic, or pepper left on the plate. Add the wine, turn the heat to high, and deglaze the pan. When nearly all of the wine has evaporated, add the cream to the pan, swirl to incorporate pan drippings and herbs, and let the cream reduce by about a third. Season with salt and pepper, pour the sauce over the tomatoes, garnish with sprigs of fresh herbs, and serve immediately.

ꙮ Fried Green Tomatoes with Cream, Bacon, & Cilantro

Serves 4 to 6

This is my favorite version of what has become, if not a truly classic dish, certainly a cliché of the times, thanks to the movie.

3 slices of bacon
4 medium green (unripe) tomatoes
5 ounce log of chèvre (chabis)
1 cup fine-ground corn-meal

Kosher salt and freshly ground pepper
$1/2$ cup heavy cream
$1/4$ cup chopped fresh cilantro

Fry the bacon in a heavy skillet until it is golden brown. Transfer it to absorbent paper. Cut and discard the stems and blossom ends of the tomatoes and cut each tomato into $1/2$-inch thick slices. Let the sliced tomatoes rest on absorbent paper or a tea towel. Slice the goat cheese into thin rounds and set it aside.

Mix together the cornmeal, salt, and pepper and dredge each slice of tomato in the mixture. Drain off all but 4 tablespoons of bacon fat and fry the tomatoes in the remaining fat over medium heat until the cornmeal browns, about $1 1/2$ minutes on each side. After turning the tomato slices once, top each with a round of goat cheese and place the pan in a 300°F oven. Crumble the bacon. After 5 minutes, remove the tomatoes from the oven and transfer them to a warmed serving plate.

Working quickly, pour the cream into the frying pan, place it over medium heat, and swirl the pan until the cream is hot but not boiling. Taste and season with salt and pepper as needed. Strain the sauce directly onto the platter of tomatoes. Sprinkle the cilantro and crumbled bacon over the surface and serve immediately.

🧄 Tomato Gratin with Fresh Basil

Serves 4 to 6

Here we have summer comfort food at its best.

6 medium ripe tomatoes, cored and sliced $3/8$ inch thick	6 leaves fresh basil, finely minced, plus 1 sprig
$1/2$ cup heavy cream	Kosher salt and freshly ground black pepper
	$3/4$ cup fresh bread crumbs

Arrange the tomatoes in a single layer in a low baking dish, overlapping them slightly so that they will fit. Set the tomatoes aside. Place the cream in a small, heavy saucepan, add the sprig of basil, and reduce the cream by half over high heat, watching it closely so that it doesn't boil over.

Remove the reduced cream from the heat and discard the basil sprig. Spoon the cream over the tomatoes, season with a little salt and pepper, and then scatter the bread crumbs over the surface. Sprinkle the basil over the tomatoes and place them in a preheated 450°F oven for about 15 minutes, until the tomatoes are tender and the juices are bubbly. Remove the tomatoes from the oven and let them sit for 5 minutes before serving.

✿ Stuffed Zucchini Blossoms

Serves 4

This recipe was developed to make use of some very ripe taupinière cheese from Laura Chenel. The filling is equally good in roasted and peeled pasilla peppers.

4 ounces taupinière, or other creamy, ripened goat cheese
4 ounces chabis or other young goat cheese
$^1/_3$ cup fresh tomato pulp (from peeled, seeded, juiced tomatoes)
Salt and freshly ground black pepper

2 tablespoons snipped fresh chives
8 to 10 zucchini blossoms
Salsa Mexicana (page 257), Summer Squash Salsa (page 267), or Rainbow Salsa (page 264)

Mix the cheeses together by hand until they are well blended. Add the tomato pulp and mix until smooth. Add salt and pepper to taste and mix in the chives. Fill each zucchini blossom with about 2 tablespoons of the mixture, just enough to fill it but not so much that the blossom can't be gently pushed closed. Chill for at least 1 hour or up to 3 hours before serving with one of the salsas alongside.

✾ Whole Roasted Zucchini with Tomato Coulis

Serves 4 as a first course, 8 as a side dish

Start picking those zucchini when they're young, before they take over the garden. This simple side dish takes very little time to prepare.

8 young zucchini, approximately 5 inches long
2 tablespoons olive oil
Black pepper
Red or Golden Tomato Coulis (pages 232–233)

Salt
Parmigiano cheese (optional)
Fresh basil, oregano, or thyme for garnish

Slice through each zucchini so that it falls open like an accordion, stopping short of cutting all the way through. Place the zucchini in a heavy, ovenproof pan, brush with olive oil, and sprinkle with black pepper. Roast the zucchini in a 375°F oven for 15 minutes, or longer if they are particularly plump. Remove them from the oven. On 4 serving plates, place 3 or 4 tablespoons of tomato coulis. Set 2 zucchini on each plate, on top of the sauce. Add a sprinkling of salt, a dusting of Parmigiano, if using, and a garnish of fresh herbs. Serve immediatley.

☙ Zucchini Ribbons in Spicy Tomato Marinade

Serves 4 to 6

This recipe works best with small or medium zucchini. The large ones fall apart and tiny, or baby, zucchini should not be sliced.

3 small or 4 medium
  zucchini
1/3 cup lime juice
1 tablespoon brown sugar
4 cloves garlic, crushed
1 or 2 jalapeño or serrano
  peppers, minced
1 teaspoon minced fresh
  ginger
2 teaspoons ground cumin
1/2 teaspoon toasted
  cumin seed

2/3 cup extra-virgin olive
  oil
4 ripe tomatoes, peeled,
  seed, and chopped
Kosher salt and freshly
  ground black pepper
1 bunch cilantro, cleaned
  and minced, with 2
  sprigs reserved for
  garnish

Cut the zucchini lengthwise—that is, end to end—in ¼-inch ribbons and lay them in a low glass dish. In a small mixing bowl, mix together the lime juice and sugar, stirring until the sugar has dissolved. Add the garlic, peppers, ginger, cumin, and cumin seed and then whisk in the olive oil. Fold in the tomatoes and season with salt and pepper to taste. Pour the marinade over the zucchini and let rest for at least an hour before grilling on a stovetop grill or over low coals. The zucchini should be cooked quickly, until they are tender and just beginning to pick up a bit of color, about 3 minutes on each side. Warm the marinade, spoon it over the zucchini, and serve immediately.

❧ Portobello Mushrooms & Roasted Asparagus with Warm Tomato-Ginger Vinaigrette

Serves 4 as a main course, 6 to 8 as a side dish

Portobello mushrooms are among the heartiest of all edible fungi, and many mushroom lovers claim they taste like steak. They are thick and rich and meaty, certainly, making them ideal as a vegetarian main course. This version pairs them with spring asparagus, roasted instead of steamed, which intensifies its flavor. The rich, gingery vinaigrette ties everything together. Serve as a main course or as an accompaniment to simple, rustic fare such as roasted chicken.

$^1/_4$ pound (1 stick) unsalted butter	Kosher salt and freshly ground black pepper
2 tablespoons fresh minced ginger	2 pounds asparagus, trimmed
2 medium red tomatoes	1 to 2 tablespoons pure olive oil
1 tablespoon finely minced shallot	1 portobello mushroom, about $^3/_4$ pound
2 tablespoons unseasoned rice wine vinegar or white wine vinegar flavored with ginger	

Clarify the butter by melting it in a heavy pan over medium-high heat and cook it until the deposits on the bottom of the pan turn a deep brown, being careful not to burn it. (At this point, the butter will smell of toasted hazelnuts and for this reason is known as *noisette* butter in France.) Remove it from the heat, skim off the scum that forms on the top, and carefully pour the butter into a heat-proof container, leaving the brown deposits behind. Add the minced ginger to the butter and set it aside. (You can prepare the butter a day or 2 in advance; refrigerate, covered, until ready to use.)

Next, make the vinaigrette. Peel the tomatoes by placing them, one at a time, on a fork and searing their skins over an open flame. Let them cool briefly, remove the skin and core, and cut the tomatoes in half horizontally. Gently squeeze out the seeds and pulp, discard them, and chop the remaining flesh of the tomato coarsely. In a small sauté pan, heat 2 tablespoons of the ginger butter, straining out any pieces of ginger, and sauté the shallot until it is soft. Add the tomatoes, sauté for about 2 minutes to heat thoroughly, add the vinegar and another 2 tablespoons of the butter, and remove from the heat. Season with salt and pepper to taste and set the vinaigrette aside. It can be made an hour or so in advance, but will need to be heated just before serving.

Lay the trimmed asparagus on a baking sheet, drizzle the olive oil over it, and toss it quickly so that each stalk is coated with a bit of oil. Sprinkle a little salt over the spears, followed by several turns of black pepper. Roast the asparagus in a 475°F oven until it is just tender, 8 to 14 minutes depending on the thickness of the spears.

While the asparagus cooks, prepare the mushroom. Trim the end of the stem and brush off any pieces of dirt. Cut the mushroom in 3/8-inch slices. Strain the butter into a heavy frying pan, heat it, and sauté the mushroom slices until they are tender, about 5 minutes on each side. Transfer them to a warmed plate.

Remove the asparagus from the oven and divide it among 6 serving plates. Add mushroom slices to each serving, placing them across the asparagus, and then spoon the warm vinaigrette over the vegetables. Add a bit of pepper to each portion and serve immediately.

☙ Stuffed Tomatoes with Six Variations

A large tomato with its insides scooped out makes the perfect edible serving dish and cooks have been filling tomatoes with all sorts of mixtures for decades. In the 1950s, tomatoes were commonly filled with cottage cheese, tuna salad, deviled egg salad, and chicken salad, all of which can still be found today, along with lots of contemporary mixtures. Many of the salads in this book, such as Lakeville Tabbouleh (page 220) and Honeyed Tomato Pasta Salad (page 221), work beautifully served in a tomato; and they are especially lovely if you can find the yellow ruffle, a nearly hollow tomato that makes a perfect serving dish. The variations here are a few of my favorite fillings for tomatoes.

BASIC TECHNIQUE:

Cut the stem end of each tomato about $1/4$ inch down, just before you get to the wide shoulder of the tomato. Discard the end and use a sharp knife to cut out most of the interior, being cautious not to cut through the side of the tomato. Use a spoon to complete the process and make a smooth interior. Set the tomatoes cut side down on absorbent toweling until ready to fill them.

TO FILL:

To fill large tomatoes, simply spoon the chosen filling into the cavity, adding enough so that it comes up a bit over the top of the tomato. If the stuffed tomatoes will be baked, place them on a baking sheet rubbed with a little olive oil.

If they will be served raw, place them on a bed of greens on a serving platter or on individual plates and add appropriate garnish.

VARIATIONS:

TINY PASTA: Mix any seed-shaped pasta (orzo, rosemarina, melone) with fresh minced herbs, extra-virgin olive oil, a little lemon juice or red wine vinegar, and crumbled feta cheese. Season to taste with kosher salt and black pepper. Fill the tomatoes and serve immediately.

BAY SHRIMP: Mix bay shrimp with diced fennel, red onion, minced chives, mayonnaise, and lemon juice. Add kosher salt and black pepper to taste and fill the tomatoes with the mixture. Serve immediately.

ASPARAGUS: Cut about a pound of fresh asparagus, trimmed, into $1^1/_2$-inch pieces, toss them with a little olive oil, and roast them in a 500°F oven until just tender, about 10 minutes. Remove the asparagus from the oven, toss with some toasted slivered almonds, and divide among the tomatoes. Place the tomatoes in a 350°F oven for 20 minutes. Remove them from the oven, top each with some Warm Tomato Vinaigrette (page 252) or Tomato Concassé (page 231), and serve immediately.

RISOTTO: Make your favorite risotto or use one of the recipes on pages 179–181, pulling it off the stove immediately after the last addition of liquid. Fill the tomatoes with the risotto, bake in a 325°F oven for 20 minutes, remove from the oven, and top each portion with a spoonful of either

Dried-Tomato Pesto (page 246) or Tomato Concassé (page 231). Serve immediately.

RATATOUILLE: Make the ratatouille on page 172. Fill the tomatoes with the ratatouille, bake in a 325°F oven for 20 minutes, and serve immediately.

POLENTA: This one takes a little more time, but the results are well worth it. Prepare 6 to 8 sturdy tomatoes for stuffing. Add $^1/_2$ cup coarse-ground polenta and 1 teaspoon kosher salt to $2^1/_2$ cups cold water in a heavy pot and set over medium heat. Stir continuously until the mixture comes to a boil, and then reduce the heat and simmer, stirring regularly, until the polenta thickens, about 15 minutes. Stir in 2 tablespoons of butter, 2 ounces (about 1 cup) grated cheese (Parmigiano, aged Asiago, or Romano), freshly ground black pepper, and 2 tablespoons of finely minced fresh Italian parsley. Continue cooking over low heat, and when the polenta pulls away from the side of the pan, remove it from the heat and let it cool for about 10 minutes but no longer. Ladle the polenta into the tomatoes, place them in a baking dish, and bake them for 20 minutes. Remove them from the oven, dust each with some finely grated cheese, garnish with a sprig of Italian parsley, and serve immediately.

SALADS

SUMMER TOMATO SALADS

A salad of fresh tomatoes—medium or large ones sliced or cut into wedges, or diminutive cherry tomatoes cut in half—made from the best-tasting tomatoes you can find, is one of the purest pleasures of summer. At the height of the season, I enjoy such a salad once a day or more, varying the additions with what is on hand and what tempts me at a particular time. The entire process, from the picking (or buying or begging) of the tomato, to its slicing and arranging on a plate, takes little time and is an entirely pleasing

activity. It is essential that you use not only the best tomatoes you can find, but those appropriate to the style of preparation. Plum tomatoes, with their dense flesh, are not well suited to salads, nor are tomatoes with large, juicy seed pockets, unless they happen to taste particularly wonderful.

✖ Sliced Tomato Salad with Eleven Variations

Serves 4

A recipe for this style of salad is not really necessary; you just need to keep a few simple rules in mind. First of all, choose 1 large or 2 medium tomatoes per person, more if the salad will be the main part of the meal. Many chefs consider it essential that you peel the tomato, but I don't make this a hard and fast rule. When I am making a simple tomato salad for myself, I don't peel the tomatoes. Nor do I peel a bushel of tomatoes when I'm serving a group of a hundred if the tomatoes are of the best quality. Thicker-skinned tomatoes have been developed for commercial reasons, for the ease of storage and shipping, and these should be peeled (actually, they should not be used at all). Salads starring unpeeled tomatoes offer up summer's simplest, rustic pleasures; but if your tastes are more refined, feel free to peel them.

Next, you must slice the tomato through its equator not through its poles—*that is, horizontally, not vertically. You are making slices, not wedges. If you look at a tomato as a tiny globe, its blossom end is the south pole, the stem end the north pole. Its fat middle is the cen-*

ter, its equator. Cut the tomato in $1/4$-inch slices parallel with the equator. Discard the pole ends and arrange the thick slices on a plate or platter.

Drizzle your sliced tomatoes with a little extra-virgin olive oil and add a sprinkling of kosher salt and freshly ground black pepper. Be sure to have plenty of good, crusty bread on hand to soak up the delicious juices that gather on the plate. And, finally, vary the color and variety of the tomatoes in each salad for a more visually striking and more delicious effect.

BASIC RECIPE:

4 large tomatoes, sliced	**Kosher salt and freshly**
Extra-virgin olive oil	**ground black pepper**

Arrange the sliced tomatoes on 1 large or 4 individual plates. Drizzle with olive oil, and season with salt and pepper. Let the salad rest for 10 or 15 minutes so that the flavors can mingle, but be sure to serve it within an hour of preparation.

VARIATIONS:

ITALIAN PARSLEY & GARLIC: Sprinkle 2 or 3 cloves crushed and minced garlic and 3 tablespoons minced fresh Italian parsley over the tomatoes before adding the olive oil.

ITALIAN PARSLEY, GARLIC, & GRATED CHEESE: Sprinkle 2 or 3 cloves crushed and minced garlic and 3 tablespoons minced fresh Italian parsley over the tomatoes before adding the olive oil. Scatter 2 ounces of grated hard cheese (Dry Jack, Parmigiano, Romano, or aged Asiago) over the tomatoes after the olive oil has been added.

TOMATOES WITH SHAVED PARMIGIANO AND GARLIC: Sprinkle 2 cloves of crushed and minced garlic over the tomatoes before adding the olive oil. Using a vegetable peeler, make 15 to 20 curls of imported Parmigiano cheese and scatter them over the tomatoes.

MOZZARELLA FRESCA & FRESH BASIL: Tuck 8 slices (about 4 ounces) of mozzarella fresca here and there between the slices of tomato before adding the olive oil. Cut 10 to 12 leaves of fresh basil into very thin, lengthwise strips and scatter them over the surface of the salad.

PEPPERS & CUCUMBERS: Before adding the olive oil, scatter 2 or 3 cloves of crushed and minced garlic over the tomatoes. Cut 2 medium or 1 large lemon cucumber into very thin slices and tuck them in between slices of tomatoes. Cut 1 medium-sized, medium-hot pepper, such as a pasilla, into thin rounds and tuck them here and there between the tomatoes and cucumbers.

LEMONS: Slice 1 lemon (Meyer's, if available) very thinly and tuck the slices here and there in between the slices of tomato before adding the olive oil.

LEMONS, CHILIES, & CILANTRO: Cut 1 lemon into very thin slices and tuck them here and there between the slices of tomato. Remove the stems and seeds and cut 1 jalapeño pepper or 2 serrano peppers into thin julienne and scatter the peppers over the surface of the salad before adding the olive oil. Add the olive oil, salt, and pepper, and then sprinkle $1/2$ cup fresh cilantro leaves over the salad.

PRESERVED LEMONS & GREEN OLIVES: Scatter $1/4$-cup thinly sliced preserved lemons (page 87) and $1/4$-cup pitted and sliced green olives over the tomatoes before adding the olive oil.

Add the olive oil, salt, and pepper, and then sprinkle with 1 tablespoon minced fresh oregano leaves.

TUNA & LEMON: Drain a 6¹/₂-ounce can of imported tuna and scatter the tuna over the tomatoes before adding the olive oil. Add 2 or 3 cloves crushed and minced garlic. Drizzle with the olive oil and squeeze the juice of ¹/₂ lemon over the salad before adding salt and pepper.

ANCHOVIES, ONIONS, & OLIVES: Peel a medium-sized sweet red onion and slice it into ¹/₈-inch rounds. Add the onion slices randomly on top of the tomatoes and then drape 6 to 8 canned anchovy fillets, cut in half, over the onions and tomatoes. Cut the fillets in half and drape them over the vegetables. Scatter ³/₄ cup pitted Kalamata, Niçoise, or salt-cured olives over the salad, and then add the olive oil, salt, and pepper.

FETA CHEESE, OREGANO, OLIVES, & ANCHOVIES: Soak 8 anchovy fillets in 2 tablespoons red wine vinegar for 30 minutes. Cut 2 ounces feta cheese into small cubes and scatter it over the tomatoes before adding the olive oil. Add ¹/₄ cup pitted and coarsely chopped Kalamata olives to the salad. Drain the anchovies, cut them in half, and arrange them over the tomatoes, cheese, and olives. Scatter the feta cheese and the olives over the tomatoes. Add the olive oil, salt, and pepper, and then sprinkle 1 tablespoon of minced fresh oregano leaves over the salad.

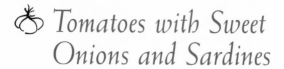 Tomatoes with Sweet Onions and Sardines

Serves 4

The culinary possibilities of sardines, tiny, softboned members of the herring family named for the island of Sardinia where they were first canned, are often overlooked. Not only are they delicious; they are also an excellent source of calcium, protein, and beneficial omega-3 fatty acids. Here they add a light yet highly nutritious and delicious element to the simple tomato salad.

4 large tomatoes, sliced
1 medium or 2 or 3 small
   sweet onions, peeled
   and cut in $^1/_8$-inch
   rounds

1 $3^3/_4$-ounce can of
   sardines, packed in
   water or olive oil
1 lemon
Extra-virgin olive oil
Salt and black pepper

Arrange the sliced tomatoes on 1 large or 4 individual plates, alternating them with rounds of onion. Carefully remove the sardines from their can, being careful not to break them. Cut the lemon in half and squeeze a bit of juice over each serving, followed by a very light drizzle of olive oil and a sprinkling of salt and pepper. Wait 10 or 15 minutes before serving so that the flavors can mingle.

 Farm Market Salad

This salad is simply a more elaborate version of a platterful of sliced, ripe tomatoes. Many years ago, I developed the habit of changing this salad based on what was at its peak at the farm market near my home, hence its name Farm Market Salad. It is a strikingly gorgeous presentation, particularly when tomatoes of varying colors are available.

10 medium or large slicing tomatoes, a mix of red, orange, yellow, and green

5 small tomatoes, about 1 1/2 inches in diameter, a mix of colors

2 cups mixed cherry tomatoes (e.g., yellow pear, red pear, Sweet 100s)

Several sprigs currant tomatoes, red and yellow

2 red onions, small torpedos if available

4 small fresh sweet peppers of various colors

4 medium lemon cucumbers

4 to 6 ounces cheese (mozzarella fresca, thinly sliced; Dry Jack or Parmesan, grated or shaved)

6 cloves garlic, peeled and minced

1/2 cup best-quality extra-virgin olive oil

Kosher salt and freshly ground black pepper

Handful fresh opal basil leaves, plus several opal basil flowers

Remove the stem and blossom ends of the medium or large tomatoes, discard the ends, and cut the tomatoes into thick (3/8-inch) slices and set aside. Cut the small tomatoes in quarters (through the poles) and set aside. Halve the cherry

215

tomatoes, cutting pear-shaped ones through the poles and round ones through the equator; set them aside. Remove any rotting tomatoes or excessive greenery from the currant tomato sprigs. Remove the root ends from the onions, peel them, and cut them into thin, round slices; set aside. Remove the stems and seeds of the peppers and cut them into thin rounds; set aside. Slice the lemon cucumbers as thinly as possible, removing the skin first if it is bruised or tough; set aside.

Assemble the salad on a large platter. Begin by placing a ring of large tomato slices on the outside edge of the plate, alternating colors and overlapping the slices slightly. Next, add a ring of onion slices, overlapping the onions onto the tomatoes by half. Add a ring of alternating tomatoes and lemon cucumbers and follow it with a ring of peppers. Continue in this fashion until all of the slicing tomatoes, onions, peppers, and cucumbers have been used. In the center of the plate, place small concentric circles of the small sliced tomatoes. If you are using mozzarella fresca, tuck slices in between tomato slices in random places. Scatter the sliced cherry tomatoes and then the chopped garlic over the salad. Drizzle extra-virgin olive oil over the surface, and add a healthy sprinkling of salt and pepper. Scatter the Dry Jack or Parmesan attractively over the salad. Add sprigs of currant tomatoes, scatter the basil chiffonade over it all, and garnish with the basil flowers. Serve immediately or cover with plastic wrap and refrigerator for up to 1 hour before serving.

🍅 Cherry Tomato Salad

Serves 4 to 6

This salad is similar to the Farm Market Salad, but with a more casual presentation because everything is tossed together.

1 quart mixed cherry tomatoes (yellow pear, gold-
   en, red, green), cut in half
6 cloves garlic, minced
1/2 cup grated cheese (Dry
   Jack, Parmesan, Asiago,
   Romano)

1/2 cup extra-virgin olive
   oil
Kosher salt and freshly
   ground black pepper
2 tablespoons snipped
   fresh chives

In a large bowl, toss together the tomatoes, garlic, cheese, and olive oil. Season with salt and black pepper, add the chives, and toss again. Serve immediately.

VARIATIONS:

PRESERVED LEMONS: Add 1/4 cup chopped preserved lemons (page 87) to the salad.

BASIL: Omit the chives; add 1/4 cup thinly sliced fresh basil leaves.

MEXICAN: Omit the chives; add 1 serrano pepper, minced, 1/4 cup cilantro leaves, chopped, and 1 tablespoon fresh lime juice.

GREEK: Use crumbled feta cheese in place of the dry grated cheese. Omit the chives and use 1 tablespoon fresh oregano instead; add 2 tablespoons finely chopped red onion and 2 tablespoons red wine vinegar.

❀ Cherry Tomatoes with Grilled Sweet Onions, Bacon, & Honey-Pepper Vinaigrette

Serves 6 to 8

This salad can be made with any onion, but it is particularly delightful with the sweet Vidalia. I also prefer it when teardrop-shaped tomatoes in orange, yellow, and red are available. Then, the salad is as visually charming as it is delicious. This is a great side dish for a summer barbecue and also excellent on a picnic.

4 medium or 2 large
   sweet onions, preferably
   Vidalia, Walla Walla, or
   Maui
Pure olive oil
3 tablespoons sherry
   vinegar
3 tablespoons balsamic
   vinegar
1/4 cup honey, warmed
1 shallot, minced
3 cloves garlic, minced

2 tablespoons freshly
   ground black pepper
1 teaspoon kosher salt
1/2 cup extra-virgin olive oil
2/3 cup pure olive oil
1/4 pound bacon, thickly
   sliced
1 tablespoon minced fresh
   Italian parsley
1 tablespoon snipped
   fresh chives
1 quart cherry tomatoes,
   various colors

Rub the onions with olive oil and grill them over medium-hot coals, turning often, until they are tender all the way through. Alternately, coat them in olive oil, set them on a rack in a roasting pan, and place them in a 325°F oven until they are tender, about 40 to 60 minutes, depending on the size of the onion. Remove the onions from the grill or oven and let them cool to room temperature.

While the onions roast, make the vinaigrette. In a medium-sized bowl, mix together the vinegars and the honey. Stir in the shallot, garlic, pepper, and salt. Whisk in the extra-virgin olive oil. Slowly whisk in the pure olive oil. Taste the vinaigrette and correct the acid/oil balance, adding more balsamic vinegar or more extra virgin olive oil as necessary. Set the dressing aside.

Fry the bacon in a heavy skillet over medium heat until it is almost crisp. Transfer it to absorbent paper to drain. Cut the cherry tomatoes in half or in quarters, depending on size, and place them in a large bowl. Discard the outer skins and cores of the onions, chop them coarsely, and add them to the bowl with the tomatoes. Add half of the vinaigrette, gently toss the salad, and taste it. Season with more salt, pepper, or vinaigrette as needed and toss the salad again. Crumble the bacon and add it, along with the parsley and chives, and toss the salad quickly a final time. Serve the salad at room temperature. If it must be kept in the refrigerator, remove it 30 minutes before serving.

 Lakeville Tabbouleh

Serves 6 to 8

For several years, I lived in a southern corner of Sonoma County, in the low, rolling hills of the dairy country known as Lakeville. It was a quiet time in the county then, with a population about 20 percent of what it is now. My young daughters thrived in the solitude, and I gardened as much as possible. My most successful crop was beautifully tender spinach. This tabbouleh, gleaned from a cookbook I can no longer recall, was one of our staples.

1 cup cracked wheat
  (bulgar)
3/4 cup extra-virgin olive oil
1/2 cup fresh-squeezed
  lemon juice
2 teaspoons kosher salt
Black pepper in a mill
2 bunches fresh young
  spinach, rinsed and
  large stems removed

2 cucumbers, peeled,
  seeded, and diced
4 stalks of celery, cut in
  small dice
6 large ripe red tomatoes,
  skinned, seeded, and
  chopped

Place the dry bulgar in a large porcelain bowl and pour the olive oil and lemon juice over it. Add the salt and a few turns of black pepper and stir the mixture briefly. Cut the spinach in thin crosswise strips and add it to the bowl on top of the bulgar. Spread the cucumbers evenly over the spinach, followed by the celery. Layer the tomatoes evenly over the celery. Cover the bowl tightly with a lid or plastic wrap and refrigerate the salad for 24 hours.

Remove the salad from the refrigerator and gently toss it, being sure to pull of the bulgar from the bottom of the bowl and to mix it thoroughly but gently into the vegetables. Taste the salad and season with additional salt and pepper if needed. Serve immediately. The tabbouleh will keep 2 or 3 days in the refrigerator but has the best flavor when eaten the first day.

🧅 *Honeyed Tomato Pasta Salad*

Serves 6 to 8

Ever since my daughter Nicolle first mixed these ingredients together one summer afternoon, we have eaten it regularly throughout the tomato season. It is at its best when the tomatoes are freshly picked from the garden.

1 pound small pasta (e.g., tripolini, small shells)
1 quart ripe cherry tomatoes or 5 or 6 ripe medium tomatoes
8 cloves garlic, minced
1 medium or 4 very small red onions, torpedo if available, thinly sliced

Handful fresh herbs (mint, oregano, Italian parsley), chopped, plus sprigs for garnish
Honey-Pepper Vinaigrette (page 218)

Cook the pasta in plenty of boiling salted water, rinse, and drain. While the pasta is cooking, cut the cherry tomatoes in half. If using larger tomatoes, remove skins by plunging the tomatoes in boiling water for 10 seconds. The skins will then pull off easily. Cut the tomatoes in half crosswise, squeeze to remove extra juice and seeds, and chop coarsely. Toss the tomatoes with the garlic, onion, and chopped herbs. Add about $1/4$ cup of the dressing, toss again, and combine with the pasta. Add the remaining dressing. Toss well and serve garnished with sprigs of herbs.

VARIATION:
Toss 8 ounces of cooked bay shrimp with a little of the dressing, add them to the salad with the rest of the dressing, and toss well.

🌸 *Pasta Salad with Cherry Tomatoes & Fresh Corn*

Serves 4 to 6

The sesame oil and rice wine vinegar join together to create an evocatively delicate flavor in this salad. Remember that all pasta salads should be served at room temperature, never chilled, and that they taste best shortly after they are made.

8 ounces dried imported pasta (small shells, tripolini, farfellini)

3 cups very small tomatoes (cherry, small pear, currant), multicolored

1 cup cooked fresh corn kernels

1/4 cup lightly toasted sesame oil

3 tablespoons low-acid rice wine vinegar

1/2 teaspoon sugar

Kosher salt and freshly ground black pepper

2 tablespoons finely minced fresh cilantro

1 teaspoon toasted sesame seeds

Cook the pasta in plenty of boiling salted water until it is just done. Rinse the pasta in cool water, drain it well, and place it in a large bowl. Cut cherry tomatoes and pear tomatoes in half but leave currant tomatoes whole; add them to the pasta, along with the corn.

In a separate bowl, mix together the oil, vinegar, and sugar. Taste the mixture and season with salt and pepper. Pour the vinaigrette over the pasta, toss the salad, add the cilantro, and toss again. Scatter the sesame seeds over the salad and serve it within an hour or so. This salad can be re-frigerated but must be removed at least 30 minutes before serving so that it can warm to room temperature.

✤ Salade Niçoise with Fresh Tuna

Serves 4 to 6

This classic salad is very popular these days, and it is never better than when it is made with fresh rather than canned tuna. If you can find one, use a delicate French olive oil in the dressing.

1 pound small red new
   potatoes
1/2 pound green beans
   (haricots verts, if
   available)
2 cloves garlic, crushed
   and minced
1 tablespoon Dijon mustard
1 teaspoon Herbes de
   Provence
1/3 cup red wine vinegar,
   medium acid
1 cup extra-virgin olive oil

Kosher salt and freshly
   ground black pepper
12 to 16 ounces fresh
   tuna, cut 3/4 inch thick
4 red ripe tomatoes, cut in
   wedges
1 small red onion, thinly
   sliced
4 hard-boiled eggs, peeled
   and sliced
Generous handful fresh
   salad greens
Currant tomato sprigs

Cook the potatoes in plenty of boiling water until they are just tender. Drain and rinse them and set them aside to cool.

Cook the green beans in boiling water, being sure not to let them overcook, and drain and rinse them. Set them aside with the potatoes to cool.

To make the dressing, whisk together the garlic, mustard, herbs, and vinegar in a small bowl. Whisk in the olive oil, taste the mixture, and season it with salt and pepper. Set the dressing aside.

Season the tuna with salt and pepper. Cook it by searing it in a very hot pan, grilling it on top of the stove, or broiling it for about 5 minutes on each side. The tuna should remain nearly entirely pink. Set it aside while you assemble the salad.

Slice the potatoes in $1/4$-inch rounds, toss them gently with a little of the dressing, and arrange them in a group on a large serving platter or 6 individual plates. Place the green beans next to them, followed by the tomato wedges, onion slices, and egg slices, reserving a space in the center of the plate for the tuna. Place a mound of greens in the center, cut the tuna into large chunks, and place it on top of the greens.

Spoon dressing over the entire salad, garnish with sprigs of currant tomatoes, and serve immediately.

VARIATIONS:

TRADITIONAL: For a traditional Salade Niçoise, omit the fresh tuna and use best-quality canned tuna, drained of its liquid.

CHICKEN: Use 1 pound of roasted chicken meat in place of the tuna, and use low-acid raspberry vinegar instead of the red wine vinegar.

🧅 Salt Cod with Summer Tomatoes

Serves 6 to 8

Make this salad only when you have superb tomatoes available. Then, all the rich flavors join together to create a sublime salad, evocative of hot summer days in the south of France. If you have never worked with salt cod before, this easy recipe is a simple way to start.

1 pound salt cod
6 or 7 small potatoes
   (Yukon Gold, Yellow
   Finn, or Red Bliss)
2 or 3 small red torpedo
   onions, peeled and
   thinly sliced

1 quart mixed small
   summer tomatoes
   (cherry, pear, currant, in
   various colors)
1/4 cup best-quality extra-
   virgin olive oil
Kosher salt
Black pepper in a mill
Aioli (page 254)

Soak the salt cod in cold water for 2 days before preparing the salad, changing the water several times to remove excess salt. An hour or two before serving, place the drained cod in a large saucepan or skillet, cover it with fresh water, and bring the water to a boil. Remove the cod from the heat, cover the skillet, and let it sit in the hot water for 15 minutes. Drain the fish well and when it is cool enough to handle, scrape off any fatty skin and remove any bones. Tear the cod into medium-size chunks and set it aside.

Boil the potatoes in their skins until they are tender

but not mushy. Drain and rinse them, then set them aside to cool.

When they are easy to handle, cut the potatoes in $^1/_4$-inch round slices and arrange them on a large serving platter. Scatter the slices of onions over the potatoes, top them with the tomatoes, and season with a few pinches of salt. Scatter the chunks of cod over the tomatoes, drizzle with the olive oil, and season with several turns of black pepper. Place the bowl of aioli in the center of the platter or serve it alongside.

❦ Bread Salad with Bacon, Tomatoes, Onions, & Olives

Serves 4 to 6

This salad evokes that great American tradition, the Bacon-Lettuce-Tomato Sandwich. If you are a stranger to bread salads in general, do not overlook them any longer. They are simply heavenly and lend themselves easily to whatever variation strikes your fancy. You must use excellent, country-style bread that is at least a day old, and you must also add enough vinaigrette dressing to moisten the bread evenly. After that, let your garden, your pantry, or your refrigerator be your inspiration. This is one of my favorite versions.

4 strips good bacon
2/3 cup extra-virgin olive
   oil
2 tablespoons red wine
   vinegar, medium acid
Juice of 1 lemon
1 teaspoon Dijon mustard
2 cloves of garlic, minced
   or pressed
Salt and pepper

4 cups day-old Italian
   bread cut in 1-inch
   cubes
1 pint ripe cherry tomatoes
1 small red onion, diced
3 tablespoons minced
   fresh Italian parsley
1/2 cup pitted Kalamata
   olives, sliced
1 quart fresh salad greens

In a heavy skillet, fry the bacon until it is just crisp. Remove
it from the skillet and let it drain on absorbent paper. Pour
the bacon drippings into a small mixing bowl, add the olive
oil, and whisk them together. In another small mixing bowl,
mix together the vinegar, lemon juice, mustard, garlic, salt,
and pepper. Whisk the oil mixture into the vinegar mixture,
taste the dressing and adjust it, adding more vinegar for
more tartness. In a large mixing bowl, toss together the
bread and most of the dressing, reserving 2 or 3 tablespoons. Let the bread sit for 30 minutes.

To serve, add the tomatoes, onion, parsley, and olives
to the bread and toss the mixture together lightly. Add the
remaining dressing, toss the mixture, taste it, and correct the
seasoning with salt and pepper if necessary. Spread the salad
greens over the surface of a serving platter and top with the
bread salad. Crumble the bacon over the salad and serve
immediately.

✤ Bread Salad with Dried Tomatoes & Capers

Serves 4

This tart and tangy bread salad is the one to make when tomatoes are out of season. It's particularly good during the holidays, when you grow weary of so much rich, festive fare.

VINAIGRETTE:

- 1/4 cup red wine vinegar (6 to 7 percent acidity)
- 1 teaspoon lemon juice
- 2 cloves garlic, minced
- 2 tablespoons minced fresh herbs
- 1 teaspoon Dijon mustard
- 3/4 teaspoon kosher salt
- 1/2 teaspoon freshly ground black pepper
- 3/4 cup extra-virgin olive oil

- 4 cups 1-inch bread cubes (see Note)
- 4 tablespoons dried tomato bits
- 2 tablespoons capers, drained of their brine
- 1/2 small red onion, diced
- 4 cloves garlic, minced
- 1 cup Kalamata olives, pitted and diced
- 2 tablespoons minced fresh Italian parsley

Make the vinaigrette by combining the vinegar, lemon juice, garlic, herbs, mustard, salt, and pepper in a mixing bowl. Whisk in the olive oil until smooth. Taste and correct the seasoning, adding more salt or pepper as necessary.

Place the bread cubes in a large bowl and toss them with half of the vinaigrette. Let them stand for 30 minutes.

Place the sun-dried tomato bits in a small bowl and cover them with the remaining vinaigrette.

Add the capers, onion, garlic, olives, and parsley to the bread cubes and toss together well. If the salad will be served immediately, add the remaining vinaigrette with the sun-dried tomatoes and toss again. If it will be held a while, wait and add the vinaigrette just before serving.

Note: Use day-old Italian, French, or other rustic bread; sour-dough is ideal.

BASIC SAUCES

🍅 Tomato Concassé

Makes about 3 cups

This is a light, uncooked tomato sauce that is full of the flavor of summer and has a multitude of uses. It can be used as the foundation of a more complex recipe, or served simply as a condiment for a variety of summer recipes, from grilled fish to risotto and tomato soufflé.

2 pounds red ripe tomatoes (not paste tomatoes) **Kosher salt to taste**

Peel the tomatoes by placing one at a time on the end of a fork and holding it over a gas flame to quickly sear the skin. Repeat until all tomatoes have been seared, let them rest and cool, and then remove the skins and stem core. Cut each tomato in half horizontally and gently squeeze out the seeds and gel. Chop the tomatoes by hand very fine and add salt to taste. Add additional ingredients—chopped shallots or garlic, fresh herbs, jalapeño peppers, lemon juice and zest, or vinegar—to resonate with the flavors of a specific dish.

VARIATION:
GOLDEN TOMATO CONCASSÉ: Use 2 pounds of ripe golden (not paste) tomatoes. After preparing the tomatoes, add 1

minced shallot, 2 cloves of crushed and minced garlic, 1 tablespoon minced fresh basil, and kosher salt to taste.

❧ Golden Tomato Coulis

Makes about 2 cups

In a coulis, the bright, fresh flavor of tomatoes is mellowed by slight cooking, resulting in a suave, refined sauce that doesn't take long to make.

6 ripe gold or yellow
  tomatoes
2 tablespoons (about $^3/_4$
  ounce) butter
2 tablespoons minced
  shallots
Kosher salt and freshly
  ground black pepper

1 tablespoon minced fresh
  basil
1 tablespoon minced fresh
  Italian parsley
1 tablespoon fresh
  snipped chives

Peel the tomatoes by placing one at a time on the end of a fork and holding it over a gas flame to quickly sear the skin. Repeat until all tomatoes have been seared, let them rest and cool, and then remove the skins and stem core. Cut each tomato in half horizontally and gently squeeze out the seeds and gel. Chop the tomatoes by hand very fine and set them aside.

Heat the butter in a heavy skillet and sauté the shallots in butter for 2 minutes; do not brown. Add tomato pulp and cook over moderate heat for several minutes until juices have evaporated and sauce thickens. Season with salt and pepper and stir in the herbs.

🧅 *Red Tomato Coulis*

Makes about 4 to 6 cups

Here's a slightly heartier version than Golden Tomato Coulis.

6 pounds ripe tomatoes, peeled, seeded, and chopped
1 tablespoon sugar
3 tablespoons olive oil
2 yellow onions, peeled and chopped
2 teaspoons minced garlic

5 basil leaves, finely chopped
Several sprigs Italian parsley
1 bay leaf
Kosher salt and freshly ground black pepper

Bring tomatoes and sugar to boil in a nonreactive stock pot. Simmer for 10 minutes and then transfer the tomatoes to a fine strainer lined with cheesecloth. Let excess liquid drain for 10 minutes and reserve it for another use. Return the drained tomato pulp to the pot and simmer over low heat until all the liquid has evaporated. Meanwhile, heat the olive oil in a heavy skillet and sauté the onions until they are soft and fragrant, about 10 minutes. Add the garlic, basil, parsley, and bay leaf and sauté another 2 minutes. Stir in the cooked tomato pulp. Taste the sauce and add salt and pepper as needed. For a completely smooth sauce, pass the sauce through a food mill. This sauce will keep, properly refrigerated, for up to a week and it can be frozen.

✿ Fresh Tomato Sauce with Butter

Makes about 2 cups

This is the simplest of the classic Italian tomato sauces. It has a rich and delicate element contributed by the butter, and is best served with delicate pastas, such as thin, handmade ravioli filled with sautéed garlic and spinach or, perhaps, morel mushrooms. It is also outstanding with classic potato gnocchi. Just be sure to top the finished dish with a healthy grating of imported Parmigiano cheese.

6 tablespoons unsalted butter	10 to 12 ripe Roma tomatoes, cored, peeled, and seeded
1 yellow onion, peeled and chopped	Kosher salt

Heat the butter in a heavy skillet and sauté the onions over medium heat until they are soft and fragrant, being careful not to let them or the butter brown. While the onions cook, chop the tomatoes. Add them to the onions and cook together until the tomatoes are soft and have begun to give up their liquid, about 20 minutes. Remove them from the heat and pass the sauce through a food mill. (For a sauce with more texture, do not use the food mill.) Season to taste with salt. Serve the sauce immediately or store it in the refrigerator for up to 3 days.

✿ Tomato Essence

Makes about 3 cups

This thin, fragrant liquid is intensely flavored and perfect when you want a great deal of tomato flavor without a lot of texture. You will net about ¹/₄ cup of tomato essence for every pound of tomatoes used, so judge your proportions by the amount of essence you need. I make mine most frequently in 10-pound batches. Be sure to begin with tomatoes that have good, balanced flavor.

**10 pounds very ripe red
   tomatoes, cored and
   coarsely chopped**

Purée the tomatoes using a food mill; discard the seeds and skins. Place the purée in a large nonreactive pot and reduce it over medium heat by one half, being sure not to scorch the liquid. Strain the reduced tomatoes through a fine sieve or a strainer lined with several layers of cheesecloth. Clean the pot and return the strained liquid to it. Reduce the mixture again until you have about 4 cups. Let the tomato essence cool, taste it, and if it seems at all weak or watery, reduce again by one-half. Cool and refrigerate for up to a week. This essence may also be frozen.

✿ Smoked Tomato Sauce

Makes about 1 quart

These days, many people have small, commercial smokers, and if you have one, follow the manufacturer's instructions. But even if you don't have one, you can make smoked tomatoes by using any outdoor barbecue fitted with a cover. Tomatoes take the flavor of smoke beautifully, and sauces and soups made with smoked tomatoes have an added dimension that is quite delicious.

Hickory chips or other
    wood chips, soaked in
    water
2 tablespoons pure olive
    oil
5 pounds Roma tomatoes,
    clean but left whole

1 small yellow onion,
    minced
3 sprigs Italian parsley
Kosher salt and freshly
    ground black pepper

Prepare a charcoal fire at least $1 \frac{1}{2}$ hours before you wish to begin smoking your tomatoes. Brush the grill with a thin coating of oil. When the fire has cooled considerably from its peak of heat and the coals are completely covered with a thick coating of white ash, scatter the wet chips over the surface and the coals and quickly set the grill over the coals. The moistened chips should produce a large amount of smoke. Keep in mind that you are smoking rather than cooking these tomatoes, so make sure the fire is not too hot and that there is enough smoke being produced. Add more moistened chips if necessary.

Set the tomatoes on the grill, cover the barbecue, and close the vent on the lid nearly all the way. Check the tomatoes in about 45 minutes. They should be slightly shriveled and their skins should begin to split. If they appear done, carefully transfer them to a large bowl or pan and set them aside to cool. If necessary, leave them on the grill, covered, for an additional 15 minutes.

When the tomatoes are easy to handle, remove and discard their skins, cores, and seeds, being sure to reserve all the juices. You can store the tomatoes at this point for use in any soups, sauces, or condiments you want a smoky flavor.

To make a sauce of the smoked tomatoes, chop the pulp coarsely and pass it through a food mill. Heat the olive oil in a heavy skillet and sauté the onion until it is soft and fragrant, 15 to 20 minutes. Stir in the puréed smoked tomatoes, add the sprigs of parsley, lower the heat, and simmer the sauce for 15 to 20 minutes, until it just begins to thicken. Remove and discard the parsley sprigs, taste the sauce, and season it with salt and pepper. Serve the sauce with grilled seafood or sautéed scallops.

 Simple Roasted-Tomato Sauce

Makes about 2 cups

This sauce is based upon provençal-style baked tomatoes, and in that sense it is almost not a sauce at all, though it functions as one in a variety of recipes. The tomatoes are roasted in the oven with the traditional topping of garlic, parsley, bread crumbs, and olive oil. To work as a sauce, the roasted tomato pulp needs only to be scooped out of the shell of skin and coarsely chopped, although properly cooked it nearly falls apart of its own accord.

8 ripe tomatoes
6 cloves garlic, crushed
 and minced
3 tablespoons chopped
 fresh Italian parsley

Kosher salt and black
 pepper
2 cups fresh bread
 crumbs, toasted
Extra-virgin olive oil

Cut the stem end of the tomatoes and discard them. Set the tomatoes in a small ovenproof dish or skillet. Toss together the minced garlic, parsley, salt, pepper, and bread crumbs. Top the tomatoes with the mixture, reserving about a third of it for later. Drizzle each tomato with a healthy dose of olive oil. Roast the tomatoes in a 350°F oven for about 25 minutes, until they start to fall apart. Remove them from the oven and let them cool slightly. Use them as a sauce for seafood, roasted meats, or pasta, topping the finished dish with the remaining bread crumbs.

❧ Winter Spaghetti Sauce (Marinara)

Makes about 6 to 7 cups

There's something arbitrary, almost unnecessary, about a recipe for spaghetti sauce. Certainly, don't use mine to supplant your own. But if, for whatever unimaginable reason, you've never made spaghetti, this is not a bad way to start. Although the wine is an optional ingredient, it does add a pleasant depth of flavor, welcome if the tomatoes you are using are not the best.

Olive oil

1 medium yellow onion, diced

Several cloves of garlic, minced

¾ cup of red wine (optional)

2 28-ounce cans of crushed tomatoes

1 very small handful of fresh oregano, finely chopped

2 or 3 tablespoons chopped fresh Italian parsley

Kosher salt and freshly ground black pepper

1 teaspoon sugar

3 to 4 tablespoons of tomato paste (optional)

Heat some olive oil in a heavy skillet. Add the diced onion and sauté it over medium heat until it is transparent. Add the garlic and sauté for about 2 minutes. If using, add the red wine now and simmer it until it is reduced by half. Add the tomatoes, stir the mixture, add the oregano and parsley, and let the sauce cook over low heat for about 20 minutes. Taste the sauce, add salt and pepper, and if the tomatoes are particularly acidic, add a teaspoon of sugar for balance. If the sauce is too thin for your taste, add tomato paste, stirring in a tablespoon at a time, until the sauce is the desired consistency. Simmer it an additional 10 minutes and serve it over pasta such as spaghetti, linguine, or noodles. This sauce will keep in the refrigerator for up to 1 week. It can also be frozen for up to 3 months.

✿ *Winter Spaghetti Sauce with Beef*

Makes about 4 cups

This sauce does not really provide an adequate substitute for ragù (page 248); it is not cooked long enough to develop the richness of the traditional sauce. It is, however, a good basic sauce that is simple to put together and quick to the table.

3 tablespoons pure olive oil
1 medium yellow onion, peeled and chopped
6 cloves garlic, peeled and minced
1 pound lean ground beef

1 cup red wine
1 28-ounce can crushed or diced plum tomatoes, with their juice
Several (about 8 or 9) basil leaves, chopped

| Handful Italian parsley, chopped | 1 teaspoon kosher salt, plus more if needed |
| | Black pepper in a mill |

Heat the olive oil in a heavy skillet, add the chopped onion, and sauté it over medium heat until it is soft and transparent. Add the garlic and sauté another 2 minutes. Add the beef and crumble it with a fork as it cooks, stirring continuously until it has lost its red-raw color. Add the wine and simmer rapidly until it has evaporated. Add the tomatoes and the basil, lower the heat, and simmer until most of the liquid has evaporated, about 30 minutes. If the sauce remains fairly thin, raise the heat to medium and simmer an additional 5 minutes to thicken it. Stir in the parsley, 1 teaspoon salt, and several turns of black pepper. Taste the sauce and add more salt or pepper if necessary. Serve over hot pasta such as penne or rigatoni.

❧ Tomato Sauce with Hot Pepper and Pancetta

Makes about 3 cups

This traditional Italian pasta sauce is very appealing in its spicy simplicity. Notice that garlic is not among the ingredients. Many Italian cooks do not put garlic into their traditional tomato sauces, and my version honors the custom.

2 tablespoons butter
2 tablespoons pure olive
   oil
1 yellow onion, peeled
   and diced
4 slices pancetta, cut into
   $1/2$-inch strips

2 pounds Roma tomatoes,
   peeled, seeded, and
   chopped, or 1 28-ounce
   can Italian-style crushed
   tomatoes, with their
   juice
$1/2$ to 1 teaspoon dried
   crushed red pepper
Kosher salt

Heat the butter and olive oil together in a heavy skillet. Add the onion and sauté over medium heat until the onion is fragrant and tender, about 10 minutes. Add the pancetta, stir, and cook for 5 to 6 minutes, being careful not to brown the onions. Add the tomatoes and $1/2$ teaspoon red pepper and simmer until most of the liquid from the tomatoes has evaporated and the sauce has begun to thicken. Taste the sauce, add kosher salt and, for more heat, the remaining red pepper. Serve with hot noodles.

❀ Mexican-Style Summer Tomato Sauce

Makes about 3 cups

Rich, fragrant, and mildly spicy, this sauce is ideal for a broad range of Mexican-style dishes.

3 pounds large red ripe tomatoes	1 yellow onion, peeled, cut in quarters
2 pasilla peppers	4 tablespoons pure olive oil
2 to 6 fresh jalapeño peppers	$^1/_2$ teaspoon cinnamon
3 cloves garlic	Kosher salt and freshly ground black pepper

Place the tomatoes, peppers, garlic, and onion in a large roasting pan, drizzle a tablespoon of olive oil over them, and toss so that the vegetables are coated with a bit of the oil. Roast the vegetables in a 350°F oven for about 25 minutes, remove them from the oven, and let them cool until they are easy to handle. Stem and seed the peppers, remove the skin from the garlic, and place the chilies and garlic in a food processor. Pulse several times to break them up. Pass the roasted onions and tomatoes through a food mill and discard the tomato seeds.

Heat the remaining oil in a heavy skillet, and when it is quite hot carefully pour in the tomato-onion purée all at once, followed by the chili and garlic mixture. Stir the purée well and be sure to scrape up any sauce that has stuck to the bottom on the pan. Add the cinnamon, reduce the heat to low, cover the pan, and cook the sauce for 20 minutes, removing the lid and stirring occasionally. The sauce will be thick and very rich. Remove it from the heat and cool it slightly. Taste the sauce and season it with salt and pepper.

This sauce will keep, properly refrigerated, for up to a week and it can be frozen. Use it as a sauce for polenta, for a variety of Mexican dishes such as enchiladas and chiles rellenos, and for roast meats such as pork and beef.

🧅 Winter Tomato Sauce with Onions, Sage, & Pancetta

Makes about 4 cups

This sauce—slightly sweet from the onions and fragrant with the aroma of sage—is ideal for winter pasta dishes.

3 tablespoons butter
4 cups onions, diced
  (about 5 medium
  onions)
1/4 pound pancetta, sliced
2 tablespoons minced
  fresh sage leaves
28 ounces chopped or
  crushed canned
  tomatoes

1 tablespoon tomato paste
1 cup homemade chicken
  stock or water
1 to 2 teaspoons kosher
  salt
1 teaspoon sugar
Black pepper in a mill
Sage sprigs for garnish

Melt the butter in a heavy saucepan over medium heat. Add the onions, reduce the heat to low, and simmer slowly until the onions are soft and transparent, about 30 minutes. Meanwhile, sauté the pancetta until it is lightly browned, and then chop it and add it, along with 1 tablespoon of the sage leaves, to the onions. Stir the mixture and continue to cook it over low heat for another 10 minutes. Add the tomatoes, tomato paste, stock or water, and salt and sugar. Stir the mixture, increase the heat to medium, and simmer for 15 minutes. Taste the sauce, correct the salt and sugar, and add several turns of black pepper and the remainder of the chopped sage. Remove the sauce from the heat and either use immediately or refrigerate. When using the sauce, garnish the dish with the sprigs of sage.

🧅 *Tomato-Lemon Sauce*

Makes 1³/₄ cups

I like the pleasant tang of this simple sauce and use it often with grape leaves stuffed with rice or lamb. It takes barely any time at all to make, yet offers a great deal of flavor (and virtually no fat).

1 cup tomato sauce	2 teaspoons minced fresh
³/₄ cup homemade chicken	oregano
stock	2 teaspoons freshly
Juice of 1 lemon	ground black pepper
	Kosher salt

Heat together the tomato sauce, chicken stock, lemon juice, oregano, and black pepper. Taste the sauce and add salt if necessary. This sauce will keep for up to a week properly refrigerated.

VARIATIONS:
1. If serving the sauce with lamb, substitute lamb or duck stock for the chicken stock. Reduce the oregano to 1 teaspoon and add ¹/₂ teaspoon minced fresh rosemary to the sauce.

2. If serving the sauce with beef, use beef stock instead of chicken stock. Vary the herbs according to the herbs in the dish the sauce will accompany.

❀ Dried-Tomato Pesto

Makes about 1 pint

This savory sauce is a welcome variation of the traditional version, perfect near the end of summer when we may have had our fill of traditional spaghetti al pesto. It will freeze well, and makes not only a great sauce for pasta, but also an excellent topping for pizza, focaccia, polenta, and traditional meat loaf. When serving it with pasta, add chopped toasted walnuts, about 2 tablespoons per serving, to the final dish.

1 cup dried-tomato bits
Boiling water
1 1/2 cups (packed) fresh
    basil leaves
1/2 cup (packed) fresh
    Italian parsley sprigs
4 to 6 cloves garlic
1 teaspoon finely minced
    lemon zest

2 tablespoons butter,
    room temperature
    (optional; see Note)
1 teaspoon kosher salt
1/2 cup grated Parmigiano
    cheese
1/2 to 3/4 cup extra-virgin
    olive oil

Place the dried-tomato bits in a small container and add enough boiling water to just cover them. Let them cool to room temperature. Place the basil, parsley, garlic, lemon zest, butter, and salt in a food processor and pulse until the ingredients form a relatively smooth mixture. Add the cooled dried tomato bits and cheese and pulse again 2 or 3 times. Add the olive oil, using the full amount for a slightly looser sauce. Transfer the pesto to a bowl or jar and use immediately or store in the refrigerator for up to 10 days.

Note: I like the creaminess contributed by the butter in this recipe. If you wish to avoid the additional animal fat, simply omit it and add a little extra olive oil. Do not substitute margarine.

❦ Dried-Tomato Cream Sauce

Makes about 2 cups

This is a quick, versatile sauce that is excellent with pasta—especially fettuccine or other wide ribbons—and equally good with chicken.

2 cups heavy cream
3 cloves garlic, peeled
2 to 3 sprigs fresh thyme
2 to 3 tablespoons dried-
   tomato purée (page 56)

$^1/_4$ dry white wine
Kosher salt and freshly
   ground black pepper

Place the cream, garlic, and thyme in a heavy saucepan over medium heat and reduce the cream by a third. Discard the cloves of garlic and sprigs of thyme. Stir in the tomato purée and the wine and simmer the mixture for about 10 minutes. Season with salt and pepper to taste.

✥ Bolognese Tomato Sauce (Ragù)

Makes about 1 quart

Ragù is the richest of the Italian tomato sauces, full of a creamy depth of flavor that is unsurpassed. It is another thing entirely than the equally wonderful, quick tomato sauces that retain their fresh taste. Here, the long slow cooking mingles the flavors and textures of the various ingredients into an earthy, evocative sauce, Italian comfort food at its finest. This is the sauce that made Bologna, in northeastern Italy, famous; wherever you see alla bolognese *on a menu it refers to this traditional mixture of slowly cooked beef and tomatoes (though it is not always the real thing). It is the ideal spaghetti sauce, perfect in the winter months when we want hearty meals; it is also essential for traditional lasagne. My version is adapted from cooking teacher/cookbook author Marcella Hazan's traditional rendition.*

4 tablespoons butter
4 tablespoons pure olive oil
1 medium yellow onion, chopped
2 stalks of celery, strings removed and finely chopped
1 carrot, peeled and finely chopped

2 pounds lean ground beef
1 teaspoon kosher salt
2 cups dry white wine
1 cup milk
Generous pinch nutmeg
2 cans (28 ounces each) plum tomatoes, with their juice

Heat the butter and olive oil in a heavy, deep pot. Add the onion and sauté it over medium heat until it is soft and transparent, about 15 minutes. Stir in the celery and carrot and cook for another 2 minutes. Add the beef and crumble it with a fork as it cooks. Continue to stir the meat until it looses its raw color but has not begun to brown. Add the salt and the wine, turn up the heat, and simmer until the wine evaporates. Lower the heat, add the milk and the nutmeg, and cook gently, stirring continuously, until the milk evaporates.

Add the tomatoes, stir the mixture, and when it is thoroughly heated and begins to simmer, lower the heat and cook the sauce at the *barest* hint of a simmer for $3^1/_2$ to 4 hours. The sauce can be made 2 or 3 days in advance and reheated. It can also be frozen.

🌰 *Tomato Butter*

Makes about ¹/₂ cup

Use tomato butter with biscuits and scones, grilled seafood and chicken, or tossed with pasta as a light side dish.

2 ripe tomatoes (about ¹/₂ cup pulp), peeled, seeded, and finely chopped
1 shallot, minced
¹/₄ cup butter (1 stick), softened and cut in pieces

Kosher salt and freshly ground black pepper
1 tablespoon snipped fresh chives or 1 table- spoon finely minced Italian parsley (optional)

Let the tomatoes drain in a fine sieve for about 15 minutes, reserving the drained liquid for another use. Transfer the remaining tomato pulp and shallot to a food processor and pulse briefly to blend. Add the butter and pulse until the mixture is smooth. Add a generous pinch of salt and healthy sprinkling of pepper, along with the chives or parsley if using. Store the tomato butter in the refrigerator in a glass bowl or jar, covered, for 3 or 4 days. Let it sit at room temperature for about 30 minutes before using.

✿ Dried-Tomato Butter

This outstanding savory butter is excellent with Brie cheese and slices of baguettes. It is also excellent tossed with a variety of vegetables, including roasted asparagus, steamed green beans or broccoli, and grilled onions.

$1/4$ cup sun-dried toma-
  toes packed in oil
1 shallot, peeled
1 teaspoon fresh thyme
  leaves

Black pepper in a mill
$1/2$ cup butter, cut in
  several slices and
  softened

Place the tomatoes, shallot, and thyme leaves in a food processor and pulse until the tomatoes and shallot are finely chopped. Add a few turns of black pepper. Add the butter to the mixture and pulse until the tomato mixture and butter are combined. It will probably be necessary to scrape the sides of the processor a time or two. Transfer the mixture to a bowl or crock. Use immediately or refrigerate until ready to use. This butter will keep for about 10 days; be sure to cover it tightly between uses.

✿ *Warm Tomato Vinaigrette*

Makes approximately 3 cups

I use this vinaigrette in a variety of dishes, adding it as a topping for steamed fillets of sole, bitter greens and pasta, and risotto, to name just a few. It is simple to make and provides a great deal of flavor.

1 pound in season, ripe tomatoes
1/2 cup extra-virgin olive oil
2 or 3 shallots, minced
3 or 4 cloves garlic, minced
3 or 4 tablespoons white wine vinegar (up to 6 1/2 percent acidity)

Juice of 1/2 lemon
2 tablespoons chopped fresh herbs (basil, oregano, chives, Italian parsley, marjoram, thyme)
Salt and freshly cracked black pepper

Peel and core the tomatoes, cut them in half, remove the seeds, and chop the tomatoes coarsely. Heat 2 or 3 tablespoons of the olive oil in a heavy pan and sauté the shallots until soft. Add the garlic, sauté another 2 minutes, and stir in the tomatoes until they are heated through. Add the remaining olive oil, vinegar, lemon juice, and fresh herbs, and toss together lightly. Remove from the heat, add salt and pepper, and taste. Adjust the seasoning and acidity, adding more vinegar or lemon juice for a more tart sauce.

VARIATIONS:

TOMATO WEDGES: After peeling, cut the tomatoes into quarters. Sauté the tomatoes first, about 1 1/2 minutes on each side. Remove them from the pan to a warmed serving bowl. Sauté 1 minced jalapeño pepper along with the shallots. Toss all the ingredients together and use cilantro in place of the mixed herbs.

TOMATO-OLIVE: Add 4 tablespoons Kalamata olives, pitted and coarsely chopped, to the mixture along with the oil, vinegar, lemon juice, and herbs.

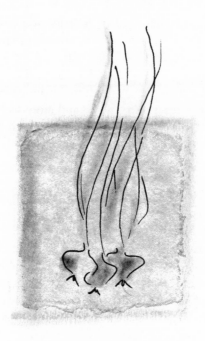

 *Aioli*

Although aioli, the pungent garlic mayonnaise of Provence, does not list tomatoes among its ingredients, it is frequently an essential accompaniment to summer tomatoes in a variety of recipes. Traditional aioli is made by hand as garlic and salt are pounded together into a smooth paste, into which fruity olive oil is added, drop by drop. This version is made quickly in the blender, and serves the grand aioli purpose quite nicely.

1 whole egg, at room
  temperature
2 egg yolks, at room
  temperature
1 teaspoon Dijon-style
  mustard or 1 teaspoon
  mustard flour
6 to 10 cloves garlic,
  peeled

¹/₂ teaspoon kosher salt
³/₄ cup extra-virgin olive
  oil
³/₄ cup pure olive oil
2 tablespoons lemon juice
  and more to taste
Pinch of cayenne pepper

Place the whole egg, egg yolks, mustard, garlic, and salt in a food processor. Process until the mixture is pulverized. With the machine running, slowly drizzle in the extra-virgin olive oil. Add the lemon juice. With the machine still running, drizzle in the pure olive oil. Taste the mixture, add the cayenne, and more salt or lemon juice as necessary. Transfer the aioli to a jar or bowl, cover it, and refrigerate it until ready to use. This aioli will keep, properly chilled, for a week to 10 days.

✿ Chipotle Mayonnaise

Makes 1 1/2 cups

Here's another condiment that contains no tomatoes, yet is a dazzling accompaniment to them. I love the deep, smoky flavor of chipotle peppers and recommend substituting this spicy mixture in a variety of recipes that call for simple mayonnaise. Experiment to find your favorite combinations.

1 whole egg, at room
  temperature
1 egg yolk, at room
  temperature
2 to 3 tablespoons red wine
  vinegar, medium acid
3/4 teaspoon kosher salt
1/4 teaspoon ground white
  pepper
1 teaspoon Dijon mustard
3 cloves garlic, peeled

2 tablespoons chipotle
  pepper purée (see Note)
1 1/4 cups unrefined corn
  oil or mildly flavored
  extra-virgin olive oil
1 to 2 tablespoons fresh
  lime juice
1 tablespoon boiling
  water, if needed
2 tablespoons finely
  minced cilantro

Place the whole egg, egg yolk, vinegar, salt, pepper, mustard, garlic, and chipotle pepper purée into a blender or food processor and process for 30 seconds. Slowly add the oil in a steady stream, continuing to process the entire time. Add the lime juice to taste. If the mayonnaise has become particularly stiff, add the boiling water to achieve the proper consistency. Add the cilantro and process very quickly, just until the herb is evenly incorporated. Transfer the mayonnaise to a nonreactive container and let it rest in the refrigerator for at least 2 hours before using it.

VARIATION:

For a quick chipotle mayonnaise, stir 2 tablespoons chipotle purée, 2 tablespoons minced cilantro, and 1 tablespoon lime juice into 1 cup homemade or best-quality commercial mayonnaise.

Note: Use canned chipotle peppers in adobo sauce and purée them, with the sauce, in a blender or food processor. The puréed peppers will keep in the refrigerator for several weeks.

SALSA

Although the Spanish word *salsa* translates into English simply as "sauce" (*sals* is an obsolete form of the English *sauce*), we think of salsa as a mildly to intensely spicy uncooked condiment that is most often, though increasingly less so, associated with Mexican and other Latin American cuisines. The chips-and-salsa duo sits on the tables of most Mexican restaurants, and market shelves are lined with scores of variations of the increasingly popular relish. Traditional salsas, as well as many innovative versions, begin with tomatoes—fresh ripe ones in season and canned tomatoes the rest of the year—or tomatillos, but the concept has been stretched to incorporate everything from watermelon, cherries, mangos, and bananas to pumpkin seeds, green olives, black beans, and minced clams. Made with good ingredients and the proper balance of heat, acid, and salt, nearly any mixture, however unusual, can be wonderful, though I prefer not to deviate too far from the original tradition. There's a point at which a salsa should be called something else.

Salsas are most often rough textured, with the ingredients cut into small to medium dice, but several traditional Mexican salsas are smooth or nearly so. In Mexico and beyond, salsas are used as condiments with egg, fish, poultry, meat, cheese, and rice dishes and, of course, on tacos. You find similar condiments, naturally under other names, in Africa, India, the Middle East, and the Mediterranean, anywhere that peasant foods are flavorful and robust and where there are plenty of fresh vegetables available.

❀ Salsa Mexicana (Pico de Gallo)

Makes about 2 cups

This is the simplest and one of the most common of the traditional Mexican salsas, and its coarse texture really makes it more of a relish. But made with ripe tomatoes it is as good with tortilla chips as it is with tacos, grilled meats and onions, and rice, anywhere at all that you want a bright, tart, savory accompaniment. If the only tomatoes you have at hand are plum tomatoes, you may need to add 3 or 4 tablespoons of water to achieve the right consistency.

3 ripe, red tomatoes, stem end removed and discarded, chopped

1 small white onion, chopped

2 or 3 serrano chili peppers, stemmed and minced

$^1/_2$ cup cilantro leaves, chopped

Kosher salt

In a medium bowl, toss together the tomatoes, onion, peppers, and cilantro. Add salt to taste and let the mixture rest at least 30 minutes before serving.

✿ Salsa Cruda

Makes 1 3/4 to 2 cups

Not quite as basic as salsa Mexicana, salsa cruda is nearly as common as an all-purpose salsa.

4 ripe, red tomatoes
1 small white onion, chopped
3 or 4 cloves garlic, crushed and minced
3 serrano peppers, stemmed and minced
2 tablespoons tomato purée
Juice of 1/2 lemon
2 tablespoons medium-acid red wine vinegar
1/4 cup extra-virgin olive oil
1/2 cup cilantro leaves, chopped
1 tablespoon minced fresh oregano leaves
Kosher salt and freshly ground black pepper

Peel and core the tomatoes. Cut them in half and gently squeeze out the seeds and excess liquid. Chop them coarsely and place them in a medium-sized mixing bowl. Add the onion, garlic, and peppers and toss. Combine the tomato purée, lemon juice, vinegar, and olive oil and pour the mixture over the vegetables, tossing to blend well. Add the cilantro and oregano and then taste the salsa. Season with salt and pepper to taste. Let the salsa sit at least 30 minutes before serving.

❦ Garlic & Chive Salsa

This one's a garlic lover's delight.

3 ripe, red tomatoes
1 small red onion, chopped
$^1/_2$ medium cucumber,
   peeled, seeded, and
   chopped (about $^1/_2$ cup)
8 to 10 cloves garlic,
   crushed and minced
2 or 3 serrano peppers,
   stemmed and minced
2 tablespoons tomato
   purée

Juice of 1 lemon
$^1/_4$ cup extra-virgin olive
   oil
4 tablespoons snipped
   fresh chives
2 tablespoons minced
   fresh cilantro leaves
Kosher salt and freshly
   ground black pepper

Peel and core the tomatoes. Cut them in half and gently squeeze out the seeds and excess liquid. Chop them coarsely and place them in a medium-sized mixing bowl. Add the onion, cucumber, garlic, and peppers and toss. Combine the tomato purée, lemon juice, and olive oil and pour the mixture over the vegetables, tossing to blend well. Add the chives and cilantro and then taste the salsa. Add kosher salt and pepper as necessary. Refrigerate the salsa for 1 hour before serving.

 # Yellow Tomato Salsa

Makes about 3 cups

Delicate and pleasing to both the eye and the palate, this light salsa is excellent on chilled poached chicken breasts and simple grilled seafood.

2 cups small yellow tomatoes (cherry or pear)
1 small torpedo onion, minced
2 cloves garlic, minced
1 serrano pepper, minced
Juice of 1 lemon

¹/₂ cup extra-virgin olive oil
¹/₄ cup cilantro leaves, chopped
Kosher salt and freshly ground black pepper

Cut the tomatoes in quarters (or smaller, if they are larger cherry tomatoes). Toss together the tomatoes, onion, garlic, and serrano pepper. Add the lemon juice, olive oil, and cilantro leaves and toss again. Season with salt and pepper and let the salsa rest for 30 minutes before serving. If you must hold it longer than 30 minutes, refrigerate it until 30 minutes before using.

 # Green Shiso Salsa

Makes about 1 1/2 cups

Jeff Dawson, who grows wonderful heirloom tomatoes for Fetzer Winery's Valley Oak Food and Wine Center in Hopland, California, gave me this recipe over dinner one night as we discussed the varieties of tomatoes he prefers. The Green Zebra, he said, is a high-acid tomato that makes a great salsa. As soon as the smallish slicer—green striped when ripe—came into season, I gave it a try. He was right; it's wonderful and it is excellent on ahi tuna, grilled very rare, just as he said it would be.

1 pound Green Zebra or Evergreen tomatoes

4 to 5 scallions, trimmed and cut in small rounds

1 serrano pepper, stem removed, finely minced

4 cloves of garlic, peeled, crushed and minced

2 to 3 tablespoons minced cilantro leaves

1 tablespoon minced shiso leaf

1 tablespoon rice wine vinegar

Juice of 1 lime

1 teaspoon kosher salt

Remove the stem ends of the tomatoes and chop them coarsely, peeling them first if you wish. In a medium-sized bowl, toss together the chopped tomatoes, scallions, pepper, garlic, cilantro, and shiso leaf. Add the vinegar, lime juice, and half the salt. Taste the salsa and add the remaining salt as needed. Let the salsa sit for 30 minutes before serving.

🌱 Grilled Tomato & Mint Salsa

Makes 1³/₄ to 2 cups

I like to make this salsa with yellow Roma tomatoes when I can find them. I like the delicate color that results, though the salsa is equally good made with red tomatoes. As with any fresh tomato recipe, just use the best-tasting tomatoes you can find.

6 to 8 plum tomatoes, red or yellow

2 to 3 serrano peppers, stems removed

1 medium red onion, minced

Juice of 2 limes

3 tablespoons extra-virgin olive oil

¹/₄ cup cilantro leaves, chopped

¹/₂ cup fresh mint leaves, cut in thin strips

2 tablespoons finely chopped fresh Italian parsley

Kosher salt and freshly ground black pepper

If possible, grill the tomatoes over hot coals or a gas grill. If not, secure each tomato, one by one, on the tines of a fork and hold it over an open flame, turning as the skins blacken. Set the tomatoes aside to cool.

When the tomatoes are easy to handle, peel and core them, and cut them in half, and squeeze out the seeds and juice. Chop the tomatoes by hand and purée half of them in a food mill. Place the chopped and puréed tomatoes in a medium bowl, add the serrano peppers, onion, lime juice, and olive oil, and toss together. Add the herbs and taste the salsa. Season with salt and pepper. Let the salsa rest for 30 minutes before serving.

🧅 Smoky Tomato Salsa

Makes 1³/₄ to 2 cups

Tomatoes easily take on the flavor of smoke, and it adds a very pleasing dimension to their taste. Tomatoes combined with the deep smoky heat of chipotles, which are ripened and smoked jalapeño peppers, make a sensational salsa that is especially good with seafood such as grilled swordfish or prawns.

8 Roma tomatoes, smoked
   (see page 236)
2 canned chipotle peppers
   in adobo sauce
1 medium red onion,
   minced
3 cloves garlic, minced
¹/₂ teaspoon ground cumin
¹/₄ teaspoon cumin seed,
   toasted

3 tablespoons red wine
   vinegar
4 tablespoons extra-virgin
   olive oil
¹/₂ cup fresh minced
   cilantro leaves
Kosher salt and freshly
   ground black pepper

Remove the stem ends of the tomatoes, peel them, cut them in half, and squeeze them to remove seeds and excess liquid. Place 2 of the tomatoes and the chipotle peppers in a blender or a food processor and purée. Transfer the purée to a medium-sized mixing bowl. Chop the remaining tomatoes and add them to the purée, along with the onion, garlic, cumin, and cumin seed. Stir in the vinegar, olive oil, and cilantro leaves and taste the salsa. Add salt and black pepper as needed and let the mixture rest at least 30 minutes before serving.

 *Rainbow Salsa*

Makes 2$^1/_2$ to 3 cups

The only reason to make this visually dazzling salsa is the availability of lots of differently colored tomatoes, the more the better. I prefer the texture of this salsa with the tomatoes peeled, but unpeeled tomatoes can be used.

6 ripe slicing tomatoes,
   each of a different color
   (whatever is available of
   green ripe, red, orange,
   yellow, pink, white,
   brown, purple, and
   marble stripe)
1 red onion, minced
2 or 3 serrano peppers
Juice of 2 or 3 limes

4 tablespoons extra-virgin
   olive oil
2 tablespoons minced
   fresh purple basil
2 tablespoons minced
   fresh mint leaves
4 tablespoons minced
   fresh cilantro leaves
Kosher salt and freshly
   ground black pepper

Core each peeled or unpeeled tomato. Cut each in half, and gently squeeze out excess liquid and seeds. Chop each tomato half separately and place them all in a medium-sized mixing bowl. Add the onion and serrano peppers and toss lightly. Add lime juice to taste, olive oil, the fresh herbs, toss again, and taste the salsa. Season with salt and pepper. Let the salsa rest at least 30 minutes before serving.

🧅 Avocado-Radish Salsa

This is one of my favorite salsas. I absolutely love the bright, crisp taste and texture contributed by the radishes. I generally eat it simply, with chips, but it is also great rolled in a warm tortilla or spooned over simple grilled or broiled tuna.

15 to 20 small radishes, chopped

1 small red onion, peeled and diced

2 or 3 jalapeño or serrano peppers, minced

2 medium avocados

Juice of 2 limes (about ¼ cup), plus more to taste

2 medium red ripe tomatoes, peeled, seed, and diced

1 bunch cilantro, large stems removed, chopped

3 to 4 tablespoons extra-virgin olive oil

Kosher salt and freshly ground black pepper

In a large mixing bowl, toss together the radishes, onion, and peppers and set the mixture aside. Cut the avocados in half, remove the seeds, scoop out the flesh, and place them in a food processor fitted with a metal blade. Add the lime juice and process until the avocado is very smooth. Transfer the puréed avocado to the mixing bowl and fold it into the vegetables. Fold in the tomato pulp, cilantro, and olive oil. Taste the salsa, season with kosher salt and black pepper, and add additional lime juice to balance the acid. Chill the salsa for at least an hour before serving.

# Grilled Corn Salsa

Makes about 2 cups

This salsa is ideal with simple cheese quesadillas or as a condiment with any grilled fish. It is also excellent in tacos made with grilled marinated steak. For festive and delicious nachos, top tortilla chips with spicy black beans and a medium-sharp grated cheese, heat in the oven until the cheese melts, and then spoon plenty of this salsa over the top just before serving.

3 ears very fresh corn
2 ripe, red tomatoes
1 small red onion, diced
2 jalapeño or serrrano peppers, with seeds, minced
1 sweet red pepper,
   trimmed and diced
1 sweet golden pepper,
   trimmed and diced

Juice of 2 limes (about $^1/_4$
   cup juice)
$^1/_3$ cup unrefined corn oil
   (see Note) or extra-
   virgin olive oil
$^1/_2$ cup cilantro leaves
Kosher salt and freshly
   ground black pepper

Remove the husks and silk from the corn and grill it quickly on an outdoor or stovetop grill, allowing it to darken slightly but not blacken. Turn the ears so the corn will cook and color evenly. Remove the corn from the grill and set it aside to cool.

Meanwhile, remove the stem end of the tomatoes, chop them coarsely, and place them in a large mixing bowl, along with the onion and peppers. Cut the kernels from the cob and add them to the other vegetables. Toss the mixture together quickly, add the lime juice, oil, and cilantro, and toss again. Season to taste with salt and pepper. Let the salsa sit for 30 minutes before serving at room temperature. It will keep, refrigerated, for 2 or 3 days, but remove it from the refrigerator at least 30 minutes before serving.

Note: Spectrum Naturals, based in Petaluma, California, produces an excellent unrefined corn oil that is rich and fragrant with the aroma of fresh corn. If you cannot locate it, use extra-virgin olive oil in its place.

❀ Summer Squash Salsa

Makes about 2 cups

It might seem unusual to make a salsa out of zucchini, but both the taste and the texture work beautifully. I like to fill ripe, Roma tomatoes, halved with their seeds removed, with this salsa, which I top with Chipotle Mayonnaise (page 255) for a spicy and refreshing appetizer in hot weather.

2 medium zucchini, 1 gold, 1 green, if available
1 small red onion
1 serrrano pepper, minced
1/4 cup Tomato Essence (page 235)

Juice of 1/2 lemon
2 tablespoons extra-virgin olive oil
1 teaspoon kosher salt
Black pepper in a mill

Cut the zucchini and the onion into 1/4-inch dice and place in a small bowl. Add the serrano pepper, tomato essence, lemon juice, olive oil, salt, and several turns of black pepper. Toss the mixture quickly, taste, and add more salt, pepper, or lemon juice if needed. Let the salsa rest at least 2 hours or overnight in the refrigerator before serving.

 *Winter Salsa*

Makes about 3 to 3$^1/_2$ cups

Yes, we should only use fresh tomatoes in their season, but there are times when one simply must have a tangy, tart salsa. What to do in the middle of, say, January when the craving hits, as it inevitably does? Use canned tomatoes—canned diced tomatoes are ideal—instead of mushy winter fruit. This version will take you all the way through a bag of tortilla chips just fine.

16-ounce can of diced tomatoes

1 small yellow or white onion, diced

1 or 2 hot peppers of choice (jalapeño, serrano, dried, etc.), minced

2 large cloves garlic, minced

3 or 4 scallions, chopped

$^1/_2$ cup tomato sauce

$^1/_4$ cup extra-virgin olive oil

Juice of 1 lemon (about $^1/_4$ cup juice)

1 bunch cilantro (about $^3/_4$ cup), chopped

Kosher salt and freshly ground black pepper

Place the tomatoes, onion, chili pepper, garlic, and scallions in a medium-sized bowl. Stir in the tomato sauce, olive oil, lemon juice, and cilantro and taste the salsa. Add salt and pepper to taste. Let the sauce rest at room temperature for 1 hour before serving.

❀ Winter Chipotle Salsa

This is a searingly hot salsa. If that worries you, use only one chipotle pepper (though I recommend you brave it through a recipe or two full strength, thereby increasing your tolerance).

3 canned chipotle peppers
   in adobo sauce
6 cloves roasted garlic,
   removed from its skin
3/4 teaspoon ground cumin
1/2 cup tomato sauce
1/4 cup extra-virgin olive
   oil
1/4 cup fresh lime juice
16-ounce canned diced
   tomatoes

1 small yellow or white
   onion, minced
1 serrano pepper, minced
2 large cloves garlic,
   minced
1/2 bunch cilantro (about
   3/4 cup), chopped
Kosher salt and freshly
   ground black pepper

Place the chipotle peppers, roasted garlic, cumin, and tomato sauce in a blender or food processor and purée until smooth. Transfer the mixture to a medium-sized bowl and stir in the olive oil and juice. In a separate bowl, toss together the diced tomatoes, onion, serrano pepper, and garlic and then fold in the chipotle mixture. Add the cilantro, taste the salsa, and add kosher salt and black pepper as needed. Let the salsa rest for at least 1 hour before serving.

ꙮ Garlic & Dried-Tomato Salsa

Makes 3 1/2 to 4 cups

This salsa is a great combination of flavors and textures. The specific ingredients and their amounts can be altered to what you have on hand—substitute a tablespoon of lemon zest for the preserved lemons, for example, or omit the walnuts or use just one type of olives. You can add things, too, like jalapeños, black pepper, or a tablespoon of mustard seeds. The most important ingredients are the olive oil (use the best you can find), the garlic (the fresher and hotter, the better), and, of course, the dried tomatoes.

3/4 cup slivered garlic
(approximately 2 heads)
2 1/2 cups extra-virgin olive
oil
1/4 cup Sonoma brand
dried-tomato bits
1/4 cup sun-dried tomatoes
in oil, finely chopped
1/4 cup chopped black
olives
1/4 cup chopped Kalamata
olives

1/4 cup capers
1/4 cup preserved lemons,
finely minced (see Note,
page 87)
1 tablespoon minced
oregano
1 tablespoon minced fresh
Italian parsley
Kosher salt
1/2 cup toasted walnuts,
chopped

To sliver the garlic, separate the cloves from the head and peel them. Slice each clove lengthwise as thinly as possible. Place the slivered garlic in a nonreactive saucepan and add enough olive oil to cover the garlic and rise $1/4$ inch above it. Simmer the olive oil and garlic over very low heat for 10 minutes, remove it from the stove, and let it cool to room temperature. Place the garlic and olive oil in a large bowl. Add all the remaining ingredients except the rest of the olive oil and the walnuts, and toss the mixture together lightly. Taste the salsa and add salt if necessary. Add the remaining olive oil. Serve as a dip or over cream cheese or chèvre. Garnish with the walnuts just before serving.

Leftover salsa must be refrigerated. Remove it from the refrigerator at least 30 minutes before serving.

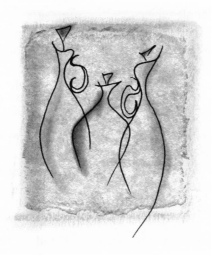

✿ Tomato Ketchup

No book on tomatoes would be complete without a recipe for America's classic condiment, ketchup. So here you have it, my version, which adds lots of depth of flavor with the addition of vanilla and cardamom.

10 pounds ripe plum tomatoes

2 yellow onions, peeled and chopped

1 head garlic, cloves separated, peeled, and chopped

2 cups pineapple vinegar or apple cider vinegar, 5 to 6 percent acidity

2 cups, packed, brown sugar

1 tablespoon hot mustard flour (or Colman's dry mustard) mixed with cold water to make a paste

2 3-inch pieces of cinnamon

1 2-inch piece of vanilla bean

1 teaspoon crushed red pepper

1 tablespoon whole black peppercorns

2 teaspoons freshly grated nutmeg

5 or 6 cardamom seeds (about 1 pod, broken open)

1 teaspoon whole cloves

1 teaspoon whole juniper berries

2 teaspoons fennel seeds

2 sprigs fresh chervil

2 sprigs fresh Italian parsley

Kosher salt

Peel the tomatoes, remove their seeds and excess juice, and chop them coarsely. Place the tomatoes in a large, heavy pot, add the onions and garlic, and bring the mixture to a boil. Reduce the heat and simmer the mixture slowly for 25 to 30 minutes.

Remove the tomatoes from the heat and let them rest and cool for about 5 minutes. Press the mixture through a food mill, discard any remaining solids, and return the purée to the cleaned pot. Stir in the vinegar, sugar, and mustard paste. Place all the other ingredients except the salt in a square made of 3 or 4 layers of cheesecloth, tie it closed, and add it to the other ingredients, pushing so that it is fully submerged. Simmer the ketchup over extremely low heat until it is thick and fragrant, about $2^1/_2$ to 3 hours. Check periodically, and skim off any foam that forms on the surface. Remove the pot from the heat and take out the cheesecloth bag. Taste the ketchup, and add a teaspoon or two of kosher salt if necessary.

Ladle the ketchup into scalded half-pint or pint jars, store in the refrigerator, or process in a water bath according to the instructions on page 279.

☙ Spicy Tomato Jelly

A spicy sweet jelly is a delightful accompaniment to many dishes—both sweet and savory. This one's great on toast, too, or with the scones on page 120.

2 cups Tomato Essence
   (page 235)
1/2 cup fresh lemon juice
3 cups sugar
2 or 3 serrano peppers,
   scored to reveal interior
   (more or less, to taste)

1 2-inch piece of cinnamon
1 2-inch piece of vanilla
   bean
3 ounces liquid pectin

In a large nonreactive pot, combine the Tomato Essence, lemon juice, sugar, peppers, cinnamon, and vanilla bean. Bring the mixture to a rolling boil and remove from the heat. Let the mixture sit for 1 hour. Discard the peppers, cinnamon, and vanilla bean. Return the tomato mixture to the heat and return it to a full boil. Add the pectin, boil 1 minute, stirring constantly, and remove from the heat. Skim off any foam that has formed on the top, ladle the jelly into scalded half-pint jars, add lids and rings, and process in a water bath for 5 minutes according to the instructions on page 279. Remove the jars from the water bath, cool them, check the seals, and store the jars in a cool, dark cupboard until ready to use.

🧅 Tomato-Onion Relish

I love sweet onions nearly as much as I love tomatoes; I can never get enough of them when they are in season, so here's a way of preserving their flavor.

3 large sweet onions (Walla Walla, Maui, or other sweet onion)	¹/₂ cup golden raisins, soaked in ¹/₂ cup balsamic vinegar
Pure olive oil	Kosher salt and freshly ground black pepper
2 cups roasted tomatoes (page 238)	

Peel the onions and cut them in half. Coat them in olive oil and grill them either over open coals, or on a stove-top grill, or roast them in 325°F oven until they are soft and tender. Remove them from their source of heat and let them cool. Place the roasted tomatoes in a strainer or sieve. Let any excess liquid collect in a bowl and either discard the liquid or reserve it for another purpose. Chop the tomato pulp and place it in a large porcelain or stainless-steel bowl. Drain the raisins and add them to the tomato pulp, along with 3 tablespoons of the vinegar. Coarsely chop the onions, add them to the tomatoes, and toss. Taste the relish and season with salt and pepper. This relish will keep refrigerated for about 2 weeks.

 Tomato-Currant Chutney

Makes 4 to 5 pints

This chutney—based on canned tomatoes—was developed out of impatience. It was the middle of winter; I wanted some tomato chutney. I decided to experiment with various canned products and was pleased with the results I got with Muir Glen's diced tomatoes.

1 pound Zante currants
1 cup balsamic vinegar
2 cups apple cider or champagne vinegar
3/4 pound brown sugar
1 2-inch piece of cinnamon
4 allspice berries
1/2 teaspoon nutmeg
1/4 teaspoon cardamom seeds

1/2 teaspoon cumin seeds, toasted
1 teaspoon hot red pepper flakes
3 tablespoons olive oil
1 medium yellow onion, minced
8 cloves garlic, minced
1 28-ounce can diced or ground tomatoes

Place the currants in a wide, heavy saucepan, cover them with the vinegars, and bring the liquid to a simmer over medium heat. Remove it from the fire, stir in the brown sugar and all the spices, and let the mixture rest for 30 minutes. Heat the olive oil in a heavy skillet and sauté the onion until it is soft and transparent, about 15 minutes. Add the garlic and sauté another 2 minutes. Add the onion and garlic combination to the currant and spice mixture, place the pan over medium heat, and simmer the liquid until most of it has evaporated and the mixture has begun to thicken. Add the tomatoes, stir, simmer 15 minutes, and remove from the heat. Spoon into hot, sterilized half-pint or pint jars to within 1/2-inch of the rim and seal jar according to manufacturer's directions. Process for 15 minutes in a boiling water bath. Store in a cool, dark cupboard for up to 1 year. You may also store the chutney in the refrigerator for up to 3 weeks.

🧄 Tomato-Garlic Chutney

Makes about 1 quart

This tangy chutney will delight any garlic lover.

3/4 cup fresh sliced garlic (about 2 heads)

2 serrano peppers, stemmed and finely minced

4 tablespoons minced fresh ginger

1 cup brown sugar

1 cup apple cider vinegar

1/2 cup balsamic vinegar

1 1-inch piece of cinnamon

1 teaspoon crushed red pepper

4 cups fresh chopped tomatoes (about 1 1/4 to 1 1/2 pounds fresh tomatoes)

1 teaspoon kosher salt

Place the garlic, minced peppers, ginger, sugar, vinegars, cinnamon, and red pepper in a heavy, nonreactive pot, stir to blend well, and simmer the mixture over medium heat for about 15 minutes, until the garlic is tender and the liquid is reduced by half. Stir in the tomatoes and the salt, reduce the heat, and simmer the chutney until the mixture thickens, about 25 minutes. Remove the chutney from heat and spoon it into hot, sterilized half-pint or pint jars to within $1/2$ inch of the rim and seal jar according to manufacturer's directions. Process for 15 minutes in a boiling-water bath. Store in a cool, dark cupboard for up to 1 year or in the refrigerator for up to 3 weeks.

PRESERVED TOMATOES

ABOUT CANNING TOMATOES

When you are selecting tomatoes for home canning, be sure to keep quality and cleaniness uppermost in your mind. After choosing ripe fruit that is still slightly firm—that is, before the dead-ripe stage—discard any tomatoes with rotten spots, lesions, or other splits. Wash the fruit very carefully in fresh water, using several rinses if the tomatoes have gathered soil from the field. Remove the cores of the tomatoes, cut away any green parts, and remove all bruised flesh. Prepare your tomatoes according to the specific recipe, always working on a clean surface and with clean utensils, and then process them as described here. For more detailed information on canning, consult one of the publications listed in the Bibliography (page 291).

Place properly sealed jars in a canning kettle half full of water, and add additional water if necessary to cover the jars 2 inches above their tops. Turn the heat to high. When the water comes to a rolling boil, reduce the heat to medium and set the timer for 45 minutes for quarts (35 minutes for pints) of whole tomatoes and tomato sauce, 20 minutes for quarts (15 minutes for pints) of tomato juice. Remove the jars from the canner and set them on racks to cool. Check the lids to be sure that they have sealed properly. There will be a slight indentation in the center of lids that have properly sealed. If one is raised, press down; if it stays down, the seal has worked. If it doesn't, reprocess the tomatoes or refrigerate them and use within a few days. Another way to be sure that the seals have worked properly is to tap on them. If the sound they make is sharp and clear, the seal is complete. If the sound is more of a dull thud, the jar is not properly closed and the product will spoil.

Once the jars have fully cooled, store them in a cool, dark cupboard until ready to use.

🌰 Canned Tomatoes, Raw Pack

Makes about 6 quarts or 12 pints

Use the best-tasting tomatoes available to you, after you have eaten your fill raw, of course. The purpose of canning tomatoes is to preserve the harvest at its peak of flavor to use during the barren months, so there is no need to can early in the season. I believe it is best to can tomatoes in as simple a form as possible, without a lot of other ingredients. That leaves you free to decide how to season each jar of preserved tomatoes as you use it. I do like tucking a basil leaf or two into jars of whole tomatoes, since basil, too, is—or should be—hard to come by in the winter months.

15 pounds of ripe red
  tomatoes
3 cups, approximately,
  freshly made tomato
  juice (page 71)

12 fresh basil leaves
1/2 cup fresh lemon juice

Have a large canning kettle ready, half full of water and on medium high heat. Peel the tomatoes (see page 44) and remove the cores. Scald 6 quart jars (or 12 pint jars) with boiling water. Pack the tomatoes, either whole or cut in wedges, into the jars, pressing to fill any spaces. Add about $1/2$ cup tomato juice if necessary (some varieties of tomatoes will have enough of their own juices) to completely fill in any spaces in the jar and to cover the tomatoes to $1/2$ inch below the top. Add 2 basil leaves (1 leaf to pints) and 4 teaspoons of lemon juice to each quart jar, half that amount to pints. Place self-sealing lids and rings on the jars. Process according to instructions on page 279.

❦ Canned Tomatoes, Hot Pack

Makes 6 quarts

This version offers a slight variation of technique.

15 pounds of red ripe tomatoes	**2 cups, approximately, freshly made tomato juice (page 71)**
12 fresh basil leaves	**$1/2$ cup fresh lemon juice**

Have a large canning kettle ready, half full of water and on medium high heat. Peel the tomatoes (see page 44) and remove the cores. Scald 6 quart jars (or 12 pint jars) with boiling water. Cut the tomatoes in wedges, place them in a large stockpot, and bring them to a boil, stirring regularly so that they do not burn. When they have boiled, pack the hot tomatoes in the scalded jars and top up the jars with the tomato juice, if necessary. Add 2 basil leaves (1 leaf to pints) and 4 teaspoons of lemon juice to each quart jar, half that amount to pints. Place self-sealing lids and rings on the jars. Process according to instructions on page 279.

 Tomato Juice

Makes about 4 quarts

Make tomato juice for canning at home if you have an abundance of particularly rich-flavored tomatoes.

10 pounds red or golden ripe tomatoes	**¹/₄ cup fresh lemon juice**
	3 teaspoons kosher salt

Have a large canning kettle ready, half full of water and on medium high heat. Peel the tomatoes (see page 44) and remove the cores. Scald 6 pint jars with boiling water. Cut the tomatoes in half and, to remove the seeds, gently squeeze them over a strainer set over a bowl. Discard the seeds and add the tomatoes and any juices collected in the bowl to a heavy, nonreactive pot set over low heat. Cover the tomatoes and let them simmer slowly for 20 minutes; remove the lid and stir occasionally so that they do not burn.

Let the tomatoes cool slightly and then press them

through a food mill. You should end up with about 12 cups of juice. Return the juice to the heat, stir in the lemon juice and salt and ladle the hot juice into the pint jars, leaving ½ inch of room at the top of the jar. Cap with self-sealing lids and rings. Process according to directions on page 279.

 *Tomato Sauce*

Makes 4 to 5 quarts

Another method of preserving the tomato harvest is to make a simple sauce.

20 pounds of red ripe
   plum tomatoes
1 cup pure olive oil
20 cloves of garlic, peeled
   and left whole

Italian parsley sprigs
Basil sprigs
¾ cup fresh lemon juice

Have a large canning kettle ready, half full of water and on medium high heat. Peel the tomatoes (see page 44) and remove the cores. Scald 8 quart jars with boiling water. Cut the tomatoes in half and gently squeeze them over a strainer set over a bowl to remove the seeds and excess moisture. Discard the seeds and reserve for another purpose the juices collected in the bowl. Chop the remaining tomato meat.

    In a heavy, wide pot heat 3 or 4 tablespoons of olive oil, enough to generously coat the bottom of the pan. Add several cloves of garlic and sauté them in the oil until the garlic is fragrant but not at all browned, about 3 or 4 minutes. Add as many of the tomatoes as the pot can comfortably hold and cook them at high heat, stirring frequently, until their liquid has evaporated and they just begin to thicken, about 5 minutes if the tomatoes are very ripe, a few minutes longer if they are somewhat firm (it takes firmer tomatoes longer to give up their water). Add 2 sprigs of Italian parsley and 2 of basil and let the tomatoes cool just slightly. Remove and discard the cloves of garlic and ladle the sauce into the scalded jars, along with the sprigs of herbs. Add 4 teaspoons of lemon juice to each quart of sauce and close the jars with self-sealing lids and rings. Repeat the process until all the tomatoes have been cooked and bottled. Process according to the directions on page 279.

 Oven-dried Tomatoes

Makes about 3 dozen dried tomato halves

This method of drying tomatoes will work best if you have a gas stove with a pilot light. Otherwise, set the controls at the lowest possible temperature.

**3 pounds (15 to 18) ripe
  plum tomatoes**

Wash the tomatoes and dry them thoroughly with a tea towel. Cut them in half lengthwise and, using your fingers, very gently scoop out the seeds and gel and discard them. Place the tomatoes, cut side up, on baking sheets and set them in a warm oven. The temperature must never rise over 165°F or the sugar in the tomatoes will burn. Leave the tomatoes in the oven until they are dry and leathery (overnight is ideal). Store them in a cool, dark cupboard and use them within 3 months. Alternately, place the tomatoes in a quart jar and cover them with extra-virgin olive oil.

PART FOUR

Appendix

Fresh Tomatoes—Purchased

Type_____ Color_____
Source_____ Cost_____
Taste_____ Aroma_____
Appearance_____ Weight_____ Acid_____
Sugar_____ Skin_____ Texture_____
Notes_____
_____
_____
Overall Opinion_____ Will Purchase Again_____

Type_____ Color_____
Source_____ Cost_____
Taste_____ Aroma_____
Appearance_____ Weight_____ Acid_____
Sugar_____ Skin_____ Texture_____
Notes_____
_____
_____
Overall Opinion_____ Will Purchase Again_____

Type_____ Color_____
Source_____ Cost_____
Taste_____ Aroma_____
Appearance_____ Weight_____ Acid_____
Sugar_____ Skin_____ Texture_____
Notes_____
_____
_____
Overall Opinion_____ Will Purchase Again_____

TASTING NOTES

Fresh Tomatoes—Home Grown

Seed Type _____ Color _____
Seed Source _____ Cost _____
Days to Maturity _____ Aroma _____
Taste _____
Appearance _____ Weight _____ Acid _____
Sugar _____ Skin _____ Texture _____
Problems & Notes _____

_____
Overall Opinion _____ Will Grow Again _____

Seed Type _____ Color _____
Seed Source _____ Cost _____
Days to Maturity _____ Aroma _____
Taste _____
Appearance _____ Weight _____ Acid _____
Sugar _____ Skin _____ Texture _____
Problems & Notes _____

_____
Overall Opinion _____ Will Grow Again _____

Seed Type _____ Color _____
Seed Source _____ Cost _____
Days to Maturity _____ Aroma _____
Taste _____
Appearance _____ Weight _____ Acid _____
Sugar _____ Skin _____ Texture _____
Problems & Notes _____

_____
Overall Opinion _____ Will Grow Again _____

TASTING NOTES

Commercial Tomato Products

**Whole Peeled • Ground • Crushed • Diced • Sliced • Stewed
Sauce • Purée • Paste**

Product_____ Brand_____
Place of Purchase_____ Cost_____
Taste_____ Aroma_____
Appearance_____ Weight_____ Acid_____
Sugar_____ Skin_____ Texture_____
Used For _____
Notes_____
_____
Overall Opinion_____ Will Purchase Again_____

Product_____ Brand_____
Place of Purchase_____ Cost_____
Taste_____ Aroma_____
Appearance_____ Weight_____ Acid_____
Sugar_____ Skin_____ Texture_____
Used For _____
Notes_____
_____
Overall Opinion_____ Will Purchase Again_____

Product_____ Brand_____
Place of Purchase_____ Cost_____
Taste_____ Aroma_____
Appearance_____ Weight_____ Acid_____
Sugar_____ Skin_____ Texture_____
Used For _____
Notes_____
_____
Overall Opinion_____ Will Purchase Again_____

BIBLIOGRAPHY

Bailey, Lee. *Tomatoes.* New York: Clarkson Potter, 1992.

Behr, Edward. "A Ripe, Flavorful Tomato." *The Artful Eater.* New York: Atlantic Monthly Press, 1992.

Bittman, Mark. "Which Canned Tomatoes Should You Buy?" *Cook's Illustrated,* March/April 1994.

Colwin, Laurie. "Tomatoes." *More Home Cooking.* New York: Harper-Collins, 1993.

Cool, Jesse Ziff. *Tomatoes.* San Francisco: Collins, 1994.

Cox, Karen. *Just Dried Tomatoes!* Westley, Calif.: Tomato Press, 1989.

della Croce, Julia. "Tomato Sauces for Pasta." *Cook's Illustrated,* March/April 1994.

Editors of Garden Way Publishing. *Tomatoes! 365 Healthy Recipes for Year-Round Enjoyment.* Pownal, Vt.: Storey Communications, 1991.

Foster, Catherine O., ed. *Terrific Tomatoes.* Emmaus, Pa.: Rodale Press, 1975.

Gould, Wilbur A. *Tomato Production, Processing, and Technology.* Baltimore: CTI Publications, 1992.

Gray, Patience. *Honey from a Weed.* Berkeley: North Point Press, 1986.

Greene, Janet, Ruth Hertzberg, and Beatrice Vaughan. *Putting Food By.* 4th ed. New York: Penguin Books, 1991.

Grewe, Rudolf. "The Arrival of the Tomato in Spain and Italy: Early Recipes." *Journal of Gastronomy,* Summer 1987.

Hendrickson, Robert. *The Great American Tomato Book.* New York: Stein & Day, 1977.

Hower, George. "High-Tech Tomato." *Press Democrat* (Santa Rosa, Calif.), September 8, 1993.

Jordan, Michele Anna. "Mutant Tomato." *The Paper* (Santa Rosa, Calif.), October 21, 1993.

Kafka, Barbara. "Tomato Times." *The Opinionated Palate.* New York: Morrow, 1992

Kummer, Corby. "Tomato Sauce," *Atlantic,* September 1988.

Lang, Jennifer Harvey. *Tastings.* New York: Crown, 1986.

Luberman, Mimi. *Terrific Tomatoes.* San Francisco: Chronicle Books, 1994.

Meyer, Scott. "Twilight Zone Tomatoes." *Organic Gardening,* March 1994.

Milioni, Stefano. *Columbus Menu.* New York: Italian Trade Commission, 1992.

Nimtz, Sharon and Ruth Cousineau. *Tomato Imperative!* Boston: Little, Brown, 1994.

Raver, Anne. "Putting Tomatoes to the Taste Test." *New York Times,* September 12, 1993.

Rick, Charles M. "The Tomato." *Scientific American,* August 1978.

Romer, Elizabeth. *The Tuscan Year.* San Francisco: North Point Press, 1989.

————. *Italian Pizza and Hearth Breads*. New York: Clarkson Potter, 1987.

Seabrook, John. "Tremors in the Hothouse." *New Yorker*, July 19, 1993.

Simeti, Mary Taylor. *On Persephone's Island*. New York: Knopf, 1986.

————197. *Pomp and Sustenance*. New York: Knopf, 1986.

Smith, Andre F. *The Tomato in America: Early History, Culture & Cookery*. Columbia: University of South Carolina Press, 1994.

Sokolov, Raymond. *Why We Eat What We Eat*. New York: Simon & Schuster, 1991.

Waldron, Maggie. *Cold Spaghetti at Midnight*. New York: Morrow, 1992.

Waltenspiels, The. *The Sonoma Dried Tomato Cookbook*. Healdsburg, Calif.: Timber Crest Farms, 1992.

RESOURCES

California Tomato Board
2017 N. Gateway, Suite 102
Fresno, CA 93727
1-800-827-0628

Florida Tomato Committee
P. O. Box 140635
Orlando, FL 32814

Georgia Giant Tomato Contest
706-722-0661
*Sponsored by Bricker's Organic
Farm, Inc., of August, Georgia, the
contest offers cash awards for the
largest tomato grown with Bricko
products. Judging in October.*

Heritage Seed Program
RR 3
Uxbridge, ON
Canada L9P 1R3
*Membership, $18.00 U.S., $15.00
Canadian; Canada's version of
Seed Savers Exchange*

Johnny's Selected Seeds
310 Foss Hill Road
Albion, ME 04910
207-437-9294
Catalog, free

Just Tomatoes Company
P.O. Box 807
Westley, CA 95387
209-894-5391
Mail-order dried tomatoes

Ornamental Edibles
3622 Weedin Court
San Jose, CA
Catalog, $2.00

Pittston Tomato Festival (PA)
717-654-0311
Anne Bradbury
*Four-day August festival features
music, food, and tomato contests
with prizes for smallest, most unusual, perfect, and ugliest tomatoes.*

Reynoldsburg Tomato Festival
   (OH)
614-TOMATO-1
*A Tomato Queen and Tomato Prin-
cess are chosen at this September
celebration honoring Alexander W.
Livingston (1821–98), a seed salesman who helped dispel the myth of
the tomato as poisonous. The event,
founded in 1973, concludes with a
parade.*

Seed Savers Exchange
3076 North Winn Road
Decorah, IA 52101
*Membership, $25.00 U.S., $30.00
Canadian; Informational brochure,
$1.00; Genetic preservation pro-
gram; members exchange seeds for a
small fee; annual yearbook lists all
available varieties*

Seeds Blum
Idaho City Stage
Boise, ID 83706
208-342-0858

Seeds Trust/High Altitude
    Gardens
P.O. Box 1048
Hailey, ID 83333-1048
*Catalog, $3.00, includes Siberian
seed stock*

Shepherd's Garden Seeds
30 Irene Street
Torrington, CT 06793
Catalog, $1.00

Southern Exposure Seed
    Exchange
P.O. Box 158
North Garden, VA 22959
804-973-4703
Catalog, $3.00

New Jersey Championship
    Tomato Weigh-In
P.O. Box 123
Monmouth Beach, NJ 07750
908-229-2395
Joe Heimbold
*Started in 1978 by a New Jersey
liquor distributor, this contest offers
substantial cash awards for the
heaviest tomatoes.*

Seed Corps
P.O. Box 1705
Santa Rosa, CA 95402
707-545-4171; fax 707-575-3707
Ian Allison, Director
Solar-start tomato greenhouse

Tomato Club
114 E. Main Street
Bogota, NJ 07603
201-488-2231; fax 201-489-4609
*Monthly member newsletter focuses
on growing tomatoes.*

Timber Crest Farms
4791 Dry Creek Road
Healdsburg, CA 95448
Ruth Waltenspiel
Mail-order dried-tomato products

Tomato Genetics Resource
Center
Genetic Resources
Conservation Program
University of California
Davis, CA 95616
916-757-8920
Charles Rick, Curator
*Major international repository for to-
mato germ plasm; collection includes
over 3,000 varieties, with about
1,000 from wild stock.*

Tomato Growers Supply
Company
P.O. Box 2237
Fort Myers, FL 33902
813-768-1119
Catalog, free

Totally Tomatoes
P.O. Box 1626
Augusta, GA 30903
fax 803-663-9772

World's Largest Tomato
3201 Rollingwood Drive
Edmond, OK 73034
Gordon Graham
*$3.50 for a copy of "How to Grow
Giant Tomatoes" by the man who's
listed in the Guinness Book of World
Records for growing the largest tomato plant ever recorded (Sweet 100,
28 feet tall, 53$^1/_2$ feet long).*

INDEX